Power Maths

Year 2
Textbook 2A

White Rose Maths ~~tion~~

Dexter

Dexter is determined.

He likes to help if you get stuck.

flexible

brave

curious

helpful

Flo

Astrid

Ash

Sparks

Series editor: Tony Staneff
Lead author: Josh Lury
Consultant (first edition): Professor Liu Jian
Author team (first edition): Tony Staneff, Josh Lury, Kelsey Brown, Liu Jan, Zhang Dan and Wang Mingming

Pearson

Contents

This shows us what page to turn to.

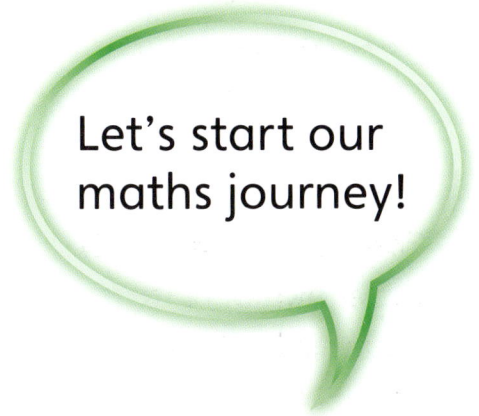

Let's start our maths journey!

How to use this book

Let's see how Power Maths works!

These pages help us get ready for a new unit.

Unit 3
Addition and subtraction ❷

In this unit we will …
- ⚡ Add two 2-digit numbers
- ⚡ Subtract 2-digit numbers
- ⚡ Find the difference between two numbers
- ⚡ Solve missing number problems

How many more rubbers are there than pencils? Use the number line to find out.

6 7 8 9 10 11 12 13 14 15 16 17 18

We will need some maths words. Do you remember any of them?

total	tens	ones
subtract	difference
10 more	10 less
bar model	represent

Base 10 equipment is useful. Use it to find the total of 16 + 7.

134

135

Discover

Lessons start with Discover.

Have fun exploring new maths problems.

Unit 3: Addition and subtraction (2), Lesson 2

Add and subtract 10s

Discover

❶ a) How many toffee apples are on the table?
How many toffee apples are on the ground?

b) How many toffee apples are there in total?

140

Share

Next, we share what we found out.

Did we all solve the problems the same way?

Think together

Then we have a go at some more problems together.

We will try a challenge too!

This tells you which page to go to in your Practice Book.

At the end of a unit we will show how much we can do!

Unit 1
Numbers to 100

In this unit we will ...
- ⚡ Count numbers to 100
- ⚡ Use different ways to show numbers to 100
- ⚡ Use place value grids to make and compare numbers
- ⚡ Compare and order numbers to 100
- ⚡ Count in 2s, 5s and 10s
- ⚡ Count in 3s

Can you work out how many there are?

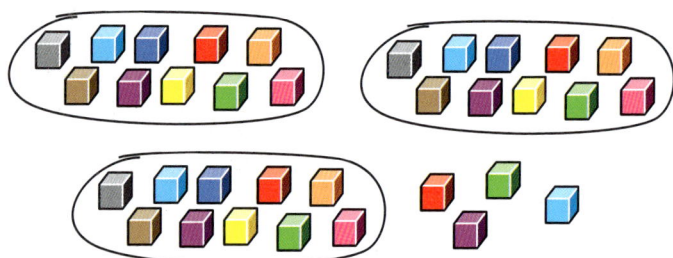

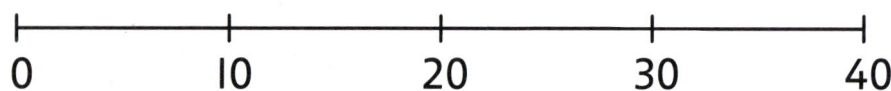

Here are some maths words you have seen before. Which ones can you remember?

tens   ones

place value grid   partition   more

fewer   fewest   greatest   smallest

We can use

T	O

to show a number. Use it to show 43.

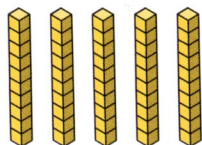

T	O

Numbers to 20

Discover

1 a) What could the mystery number be?

b) Represent 15 on a ten frame.

Share

a) The mystery number cannot be 15.

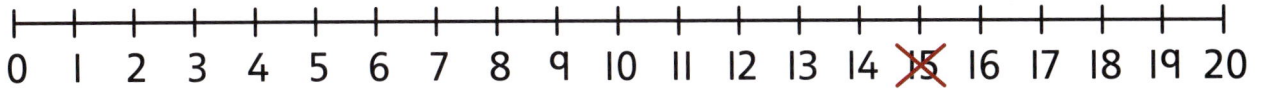

0 1 2 3 4 5 6 7 8 9 10 11 12 13 14 ̶1̶5̶ 16 17 18 19 20

It cannot be any number less than 15.

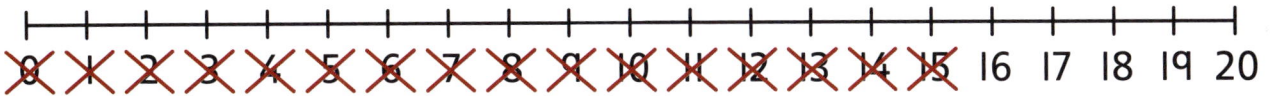

̶0̶ ̶1̶ ̶2̶ ̶3̶ ̶4̶ ̶5̶ ̶6̶ ̶7̶ ̶8̶ ̶9̶ ̶1̶0̶ ̶1̶1̶ ̶1̶2̶ ̶1̶3̶ ̶1̶4̶ ̶1̶5̶ 16 17 18 19 20

It could be any number greater than 15.

It could be any of 16, 17, 18, 19 or 20.

b)

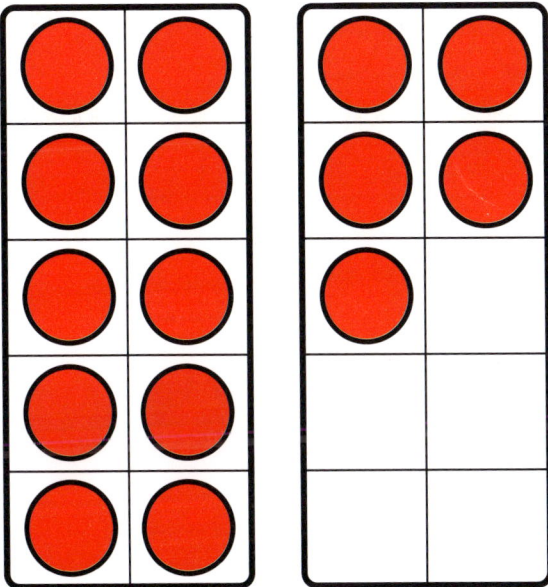

> I made the number 15 on ten frames.
> I think I could make it differently.

Think together

1 Max has some cards from 0 to 20.

Which numbers are missing?

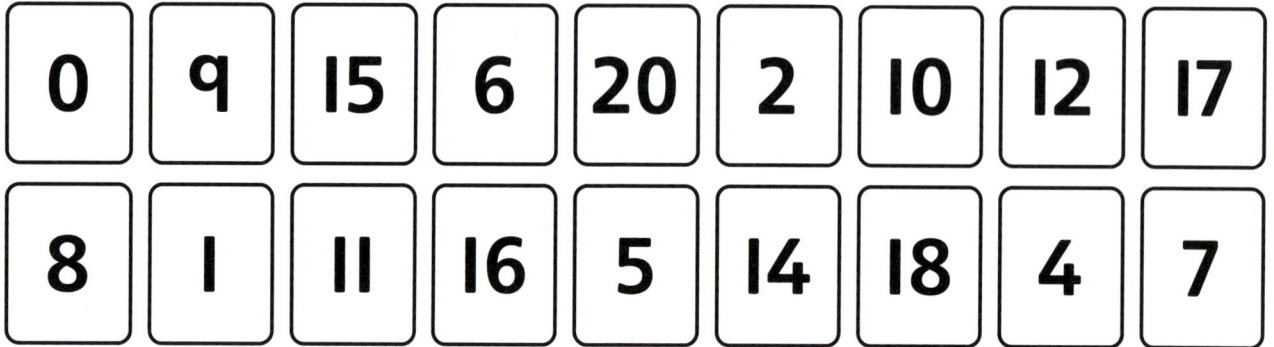

| 0 | 9 | 15 | 6 | 20 | 2 | 10 | 12 | 17 |

| 8 | 1 | 11 | 16 | 5 | 14 | 18 | 4 | 7 |

2 How many counters are in each set?

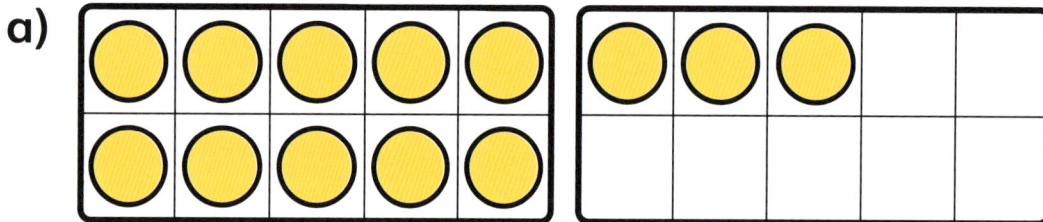

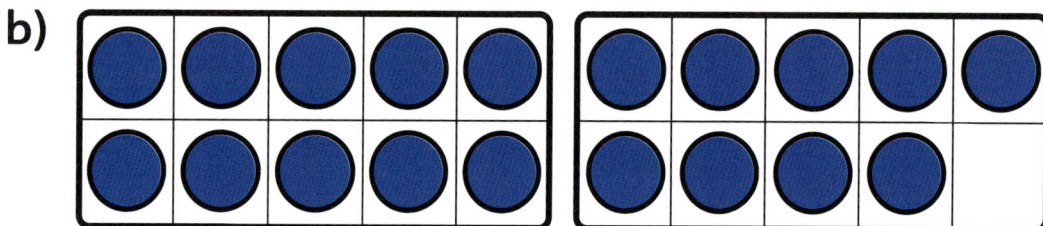

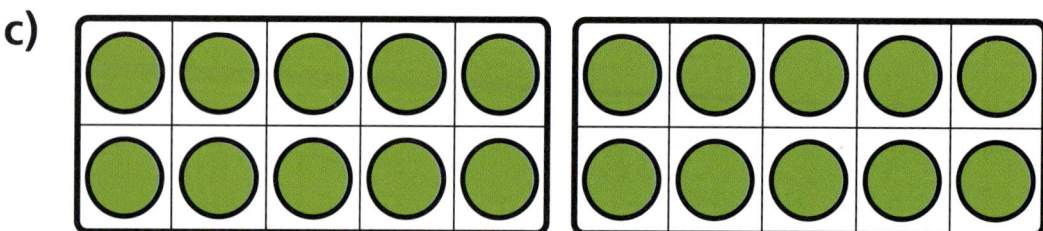

a)

b)

c)

CHALLENGE

3 Complete each part-whole model.

a)

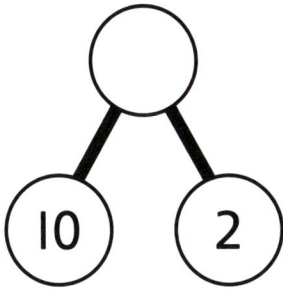

e)

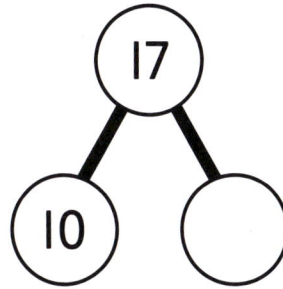

b)

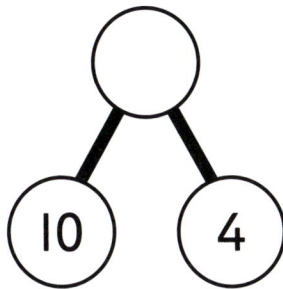

f)

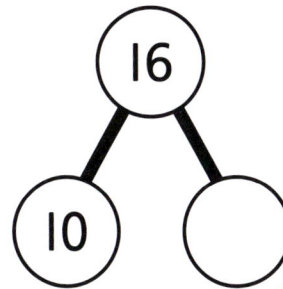

Remember that the parts add to make the whole.

c)

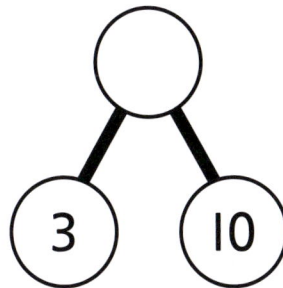

g)

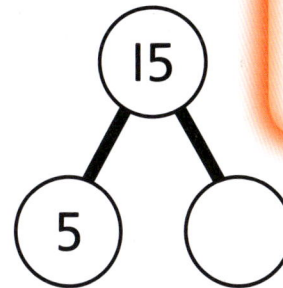

d)

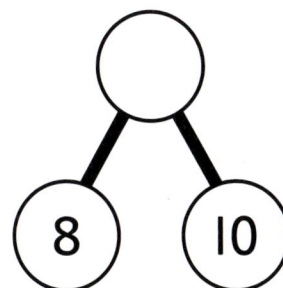

h)

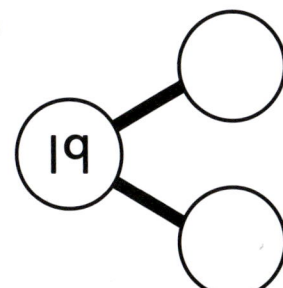

11

Count in 10s

Discover

Kara

1 **a)** How many fingers and thumbs are the children showing?

b) Kara then shows both her hands too.

How many fingers and thumbs are the children showing now?

Share

a) Count 3 **tens**.

I counted in **Is**.

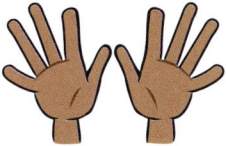 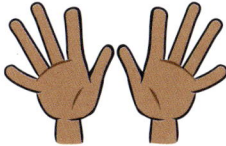 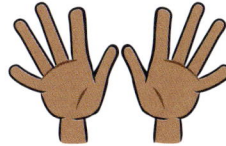

10   20   30

You can count quicker if you count in 10s.

b) Count 4 tens.

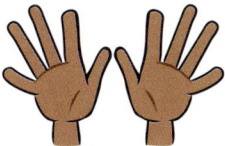 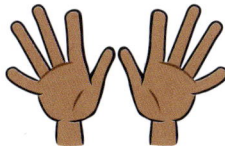 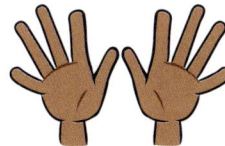 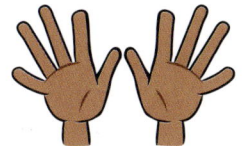

10   20   30   40

Think together

1 **a)** Count 5 tens.

b) Count in 10s.

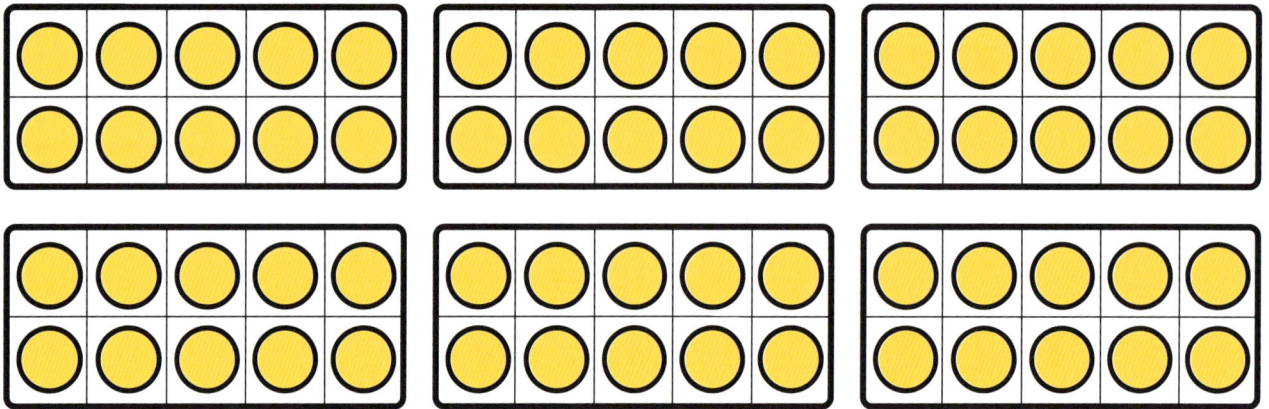

2 Complete the number track.

0	10	20			50		70			100

3 **a)** How many tens make each number?

CHALLENGE

10   [10 pencils]

20   [10 pencils] [10 pencils]

I know that 10 is 1 ten and 20 is 2 tens. I can spot a pattern here!

30   [10 pencils] [10 pencils] [10 pencils]

40   [10 pencils] [10 pencils] [10 pencils] [10 pencils]

50   [10 pencils] [10 pencils] [10 pencils] [10 pencils] [10 pencils]

b) Which number is 7 tens?

Which number is 9 tens?

How many 10s make 100?

15

→ Practice book 2A p9

Count in 10s and 1s

Discover

1 **a)** Count the stacked cones.

b) How many cones are there in total?

Share

a) Each stack has 10 cones.
Count in 10s.

10   20   30   40

I used counters on a ten frame to help me.

b) There are 3 **more** cones.
Count in 10s, then count in 1s.

10   20   30   40   41   42   43

17

Think together

1 How many stars are there?

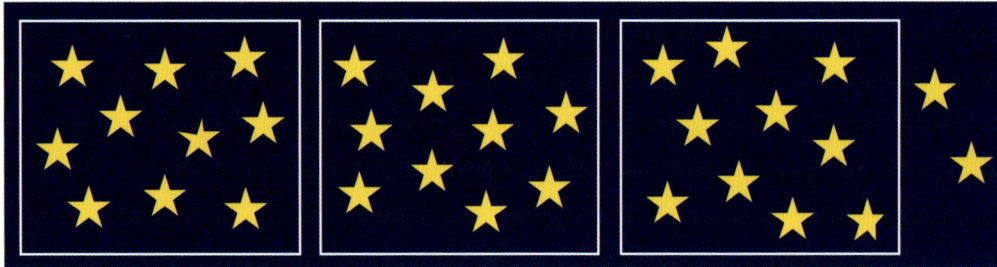

2 Are Jo and Jim correct?

a)

Jo

There are 25 seashells.

b)

I think there are 27 seashells.

Jim

CHALLENGE

3 Count the pencils, pens and rubbers.

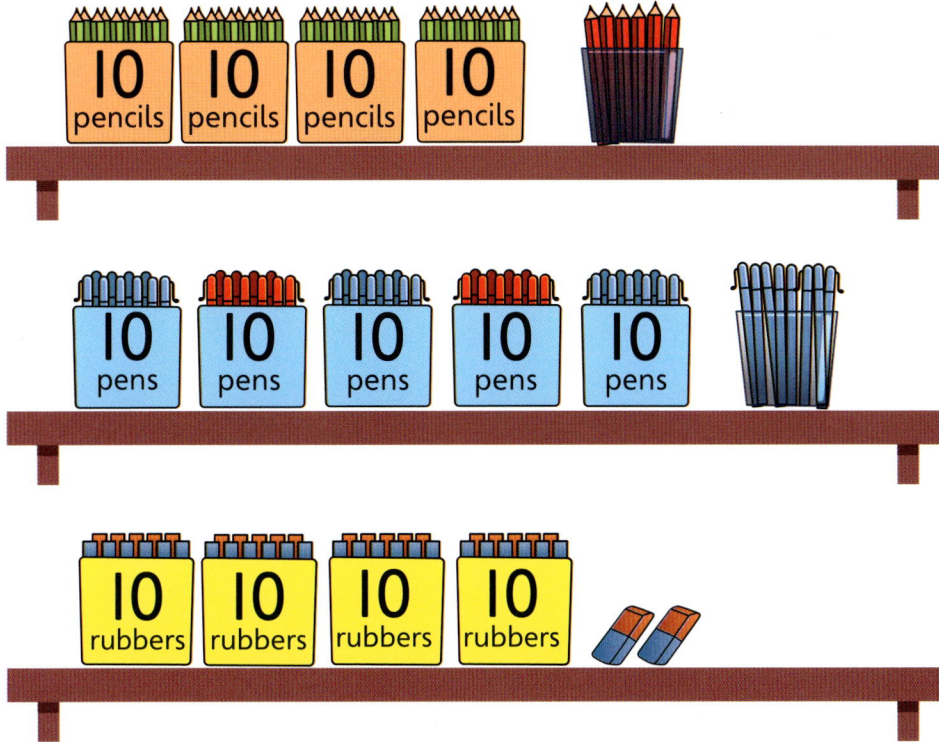

| 10 pencils | 10 pencils | 10 pencils | 10 pencils |

| 10 pens | 10 pens | 10 pens | 10 pens | 10 pens |

| 10 rubbers | 10 rubbers | 10 rubbers | 10 rubbers |

I cannot see each pencil or pen.

Let's try counting the 10s.

→ Practice book 2A p12

Recognise 10s and 1s

Discover

1 **a)** How many small cubes does Jack have?

   b) What number has Meg represented?

Share

a) Jack has 23 small cubes.

We call this base 10 equipment.

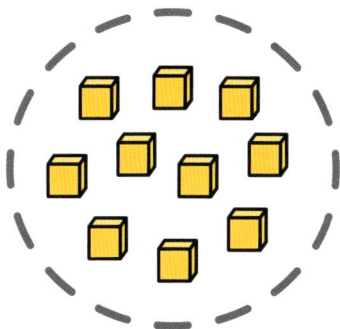 

(10) (20) (21) (22) (23)

b) The tens are shown as 10s rods.
Each 10s rod is one 10.

I know that each 10s rod is worth 10 and each cube is worth 1.

(10) (20) (21) (22) (23)

Meg has made 23.

They have made the same number.

Think together

1 Make this number from base 10 equipment.

Count in 10s and 1s.

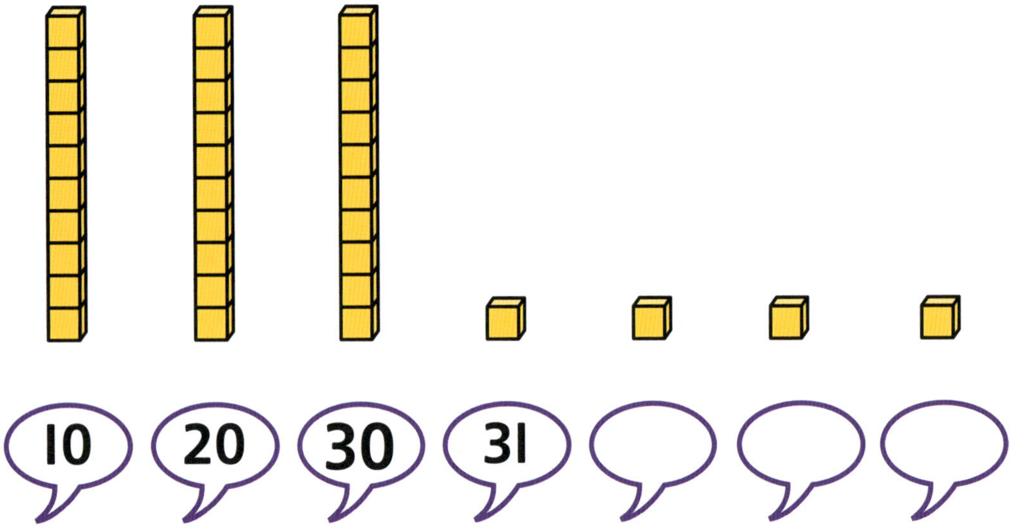

10 20 30 31 ⬭ ⬭ ⬭

2 What are these numbers?

a)

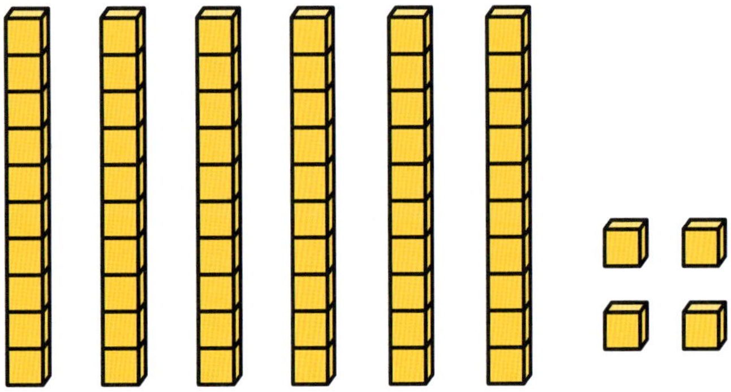

b)

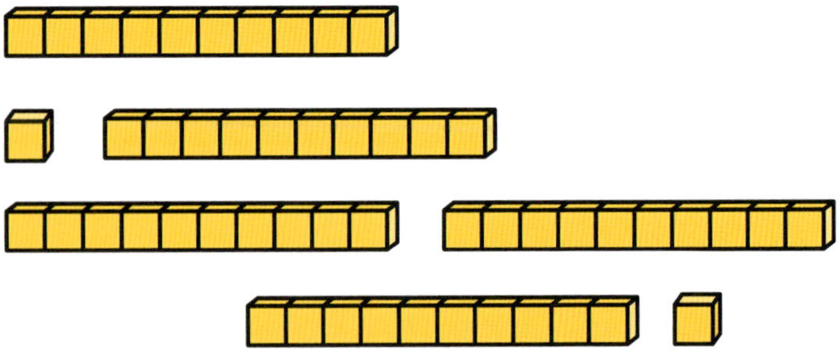

CHALLENGE

3 What is the same, what is different?

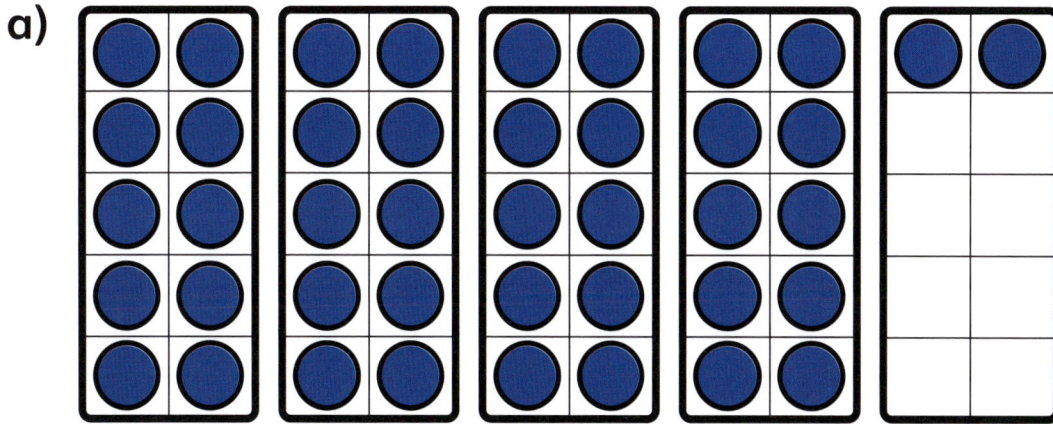

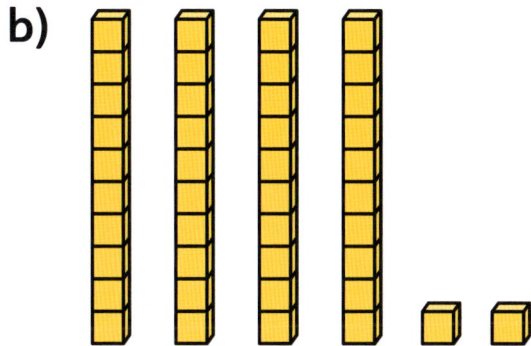

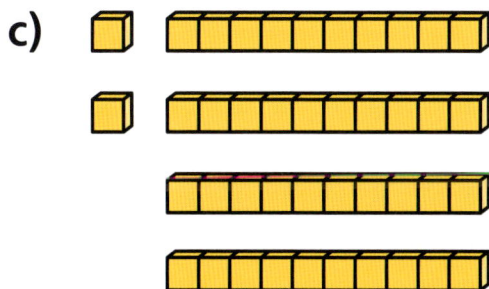

a)

b)

I'm going to work out how many 10s I have and how many 1s.

c)

→ Practice book 2A p15

Build a number from 10s and 1s

Discover

Maya

Danny

1 **a)** How can Danny build 50 from 10s and 1s?

b) How can Maya build 52 from 10s and 1s?

Share

a) Count in 10s.

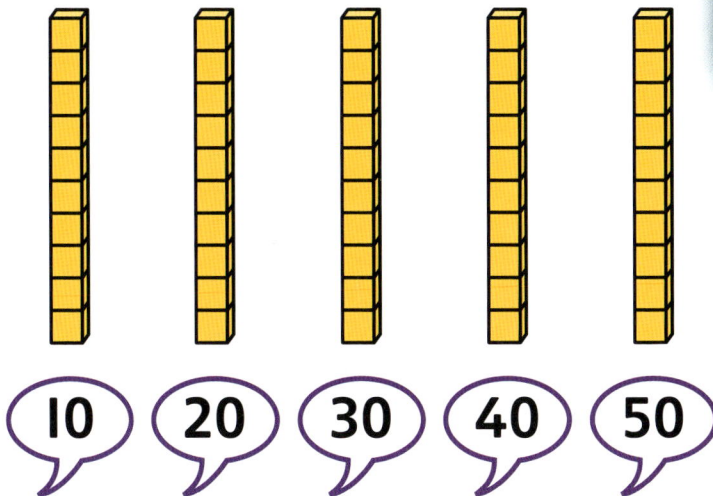

Each rod is worth 10. I remember this from the last lesson!

10 20 30 40 50

Danny does not need any 1s to make 50.

b) Count in 10s, then count in 1s.

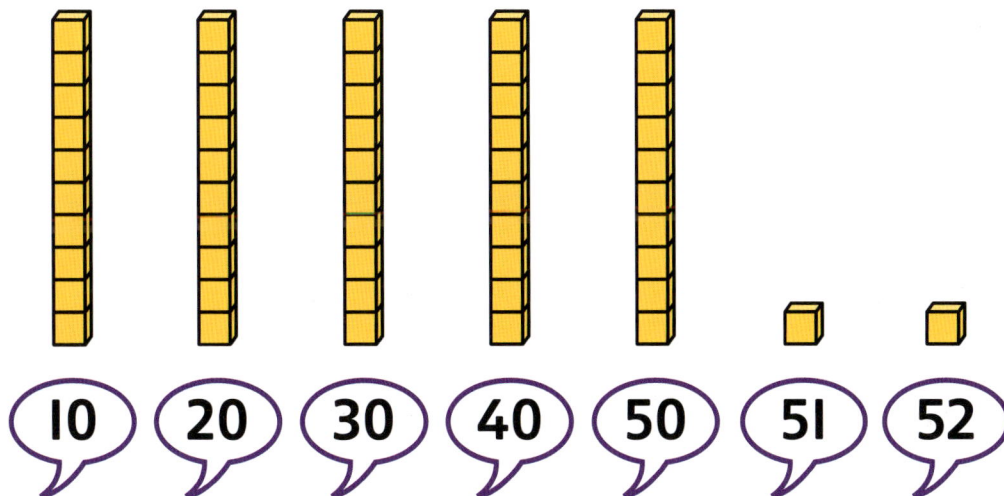

10 20 30 40 50 51 52

Maya needs 5 tens and 2 ones to make 52.

Think together

1 a) Draw or make 70.

   b) Draw or make 72.

I will draw lines and dots to represent each 10 and 1.

I know that 72 is 7 tens and some 1s.

2 Draw or make 40 like this.

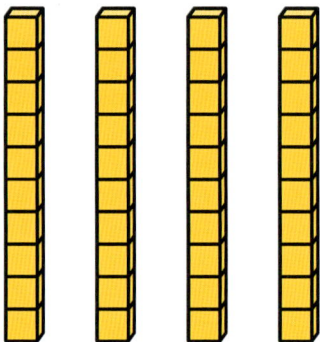

Now change it to make 41, 42, 43, 44 and 45.

I wonder if I need to add more 10s or 1s.

CHALLENGE

3 **a)**

Mr Chabra

What number has 6 tens and 4 ones?

b)

What number has 8 tens and 7 ones?

Miss Hill

I will use base 10 equipment to help me.

I will count in 10s then 1s.

27

Use a place value grid

Discover

45	50	32
30	62	23
55	56	60

What is my number? It has 3 tens and 2 ones.

Mr Taylor

1 **a)** Which number has Mr Taylor chosen?

b) What is the value of each digit in his number?

Share

a) 3 tens are 30.

2 ones are 2.

45	50	32
30	62	23
55	56	60

Mr Taylor's number is 32.

> I used base 10 equipment to help me.

b) The 3 stands for 3 tens.

The 2 stands for 2 ones.

T	O
3	2

> This is a **place value grid**. It organises 10s and 1s.

Think together

① Make these numbers using place value grids.

45, 50, 55

What does 5 stand for in each number?

T	O

② What numbers are in the place value grids?

a)

T	O

c)

T	O

b)

T	O

3 Mia has 6 digit cards.

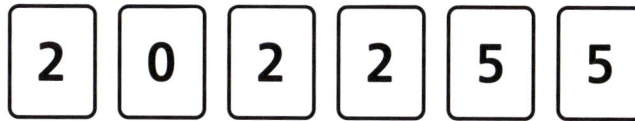

CHALLENGE

| 2 | 0 | 2 | 2 | 5 | 5 |

She makes 3 different numbers using all the cards.

T	O
2	0

T	O
2	2

T	O
5	5

Make 3 more numbers using all the cards.

T	O

T	O

T	O

I made 02. I'm not sure that's a number!

02 means no tens and 2 ones, so I think 02 is the same as 2.

31

→ Practice book 2A p21

Partition numbers to 100

Discover

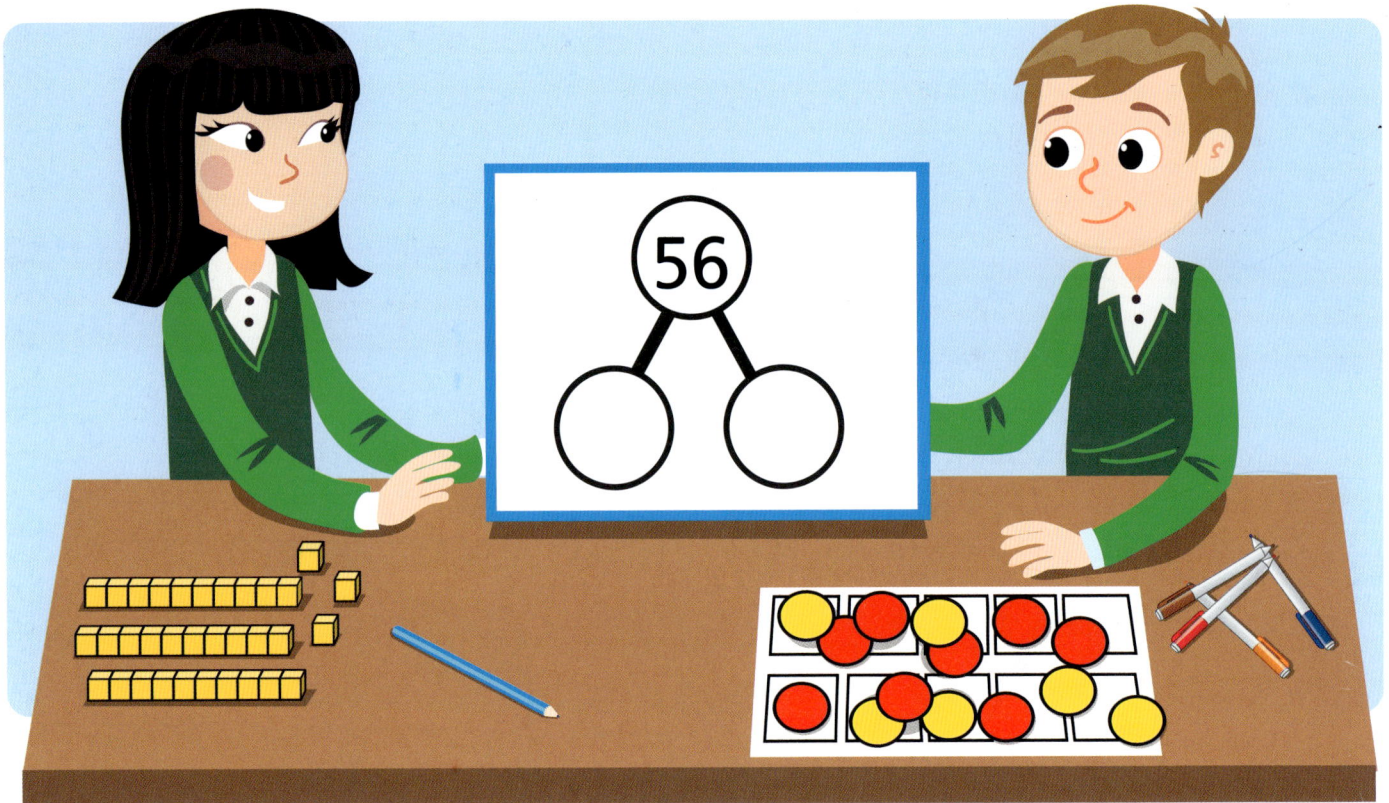

1 a) Make 56 using base 10 equipment.

b) What numbers go into the part-whole model?

Share

a)

56 is made up of 5 tens and 6 ones.

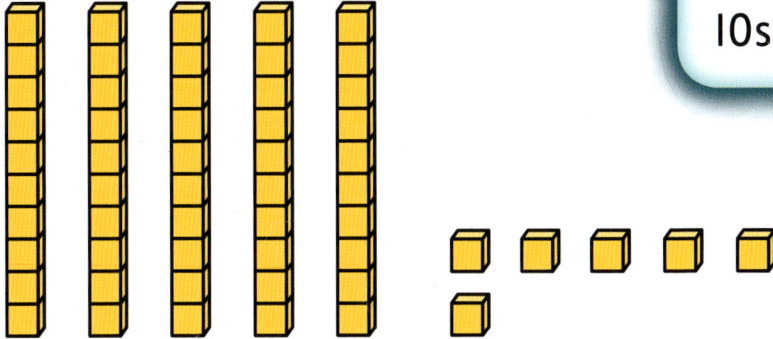

I made 56 as 10s and 1s.

b)

56

50   6

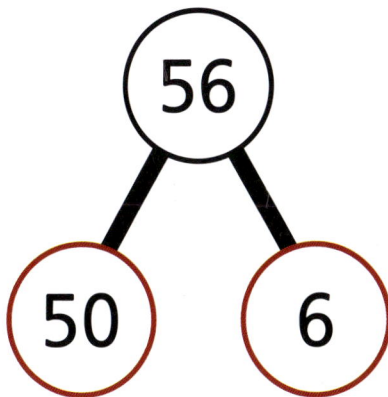

The numbers 50 and 6 go in the part-whole model.

This is an example of **partitioning** a number.

Think together

① Complete the part-whole model.

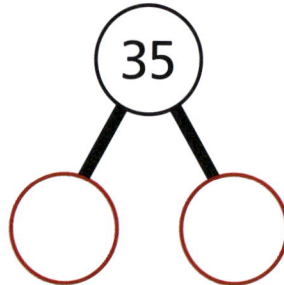

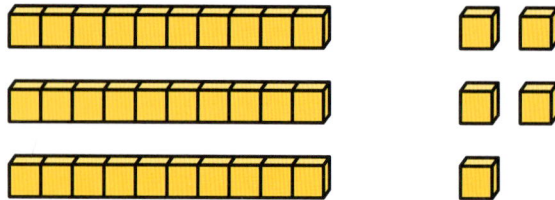

② Find the whole.

a)
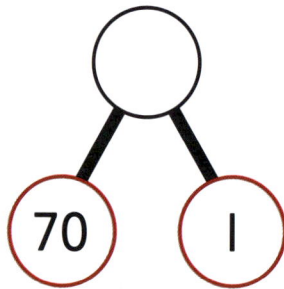

b)
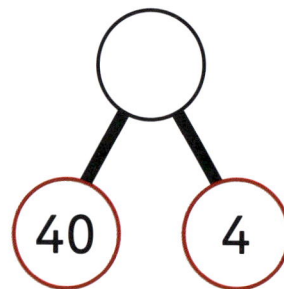

I can make these numbers using base 10 equipment.

34

3 Some numbers have been partitioned.

Which ones are correct?

What mistakes have been made?

CHALLENGE

a)
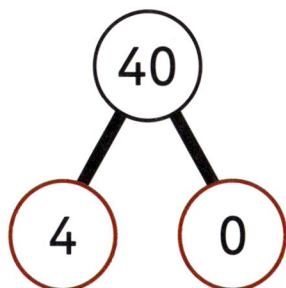

40
/   \
4   0

c)
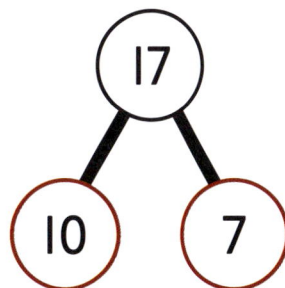

17
/   \
10   7

b)
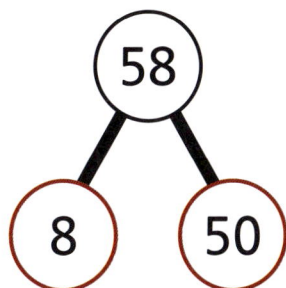

58
/   \
8   50

d)
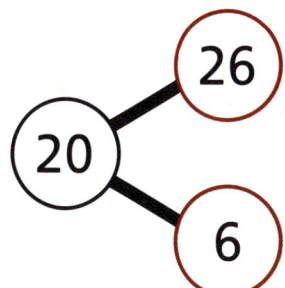

20
/   \
26
6

I will use some 10s rods and 1s cubes to check.

For the last one I wonder if the whole is in the right place.

35

→ Practice book 2A p24

Partition numbers flexibly within 100

Discover

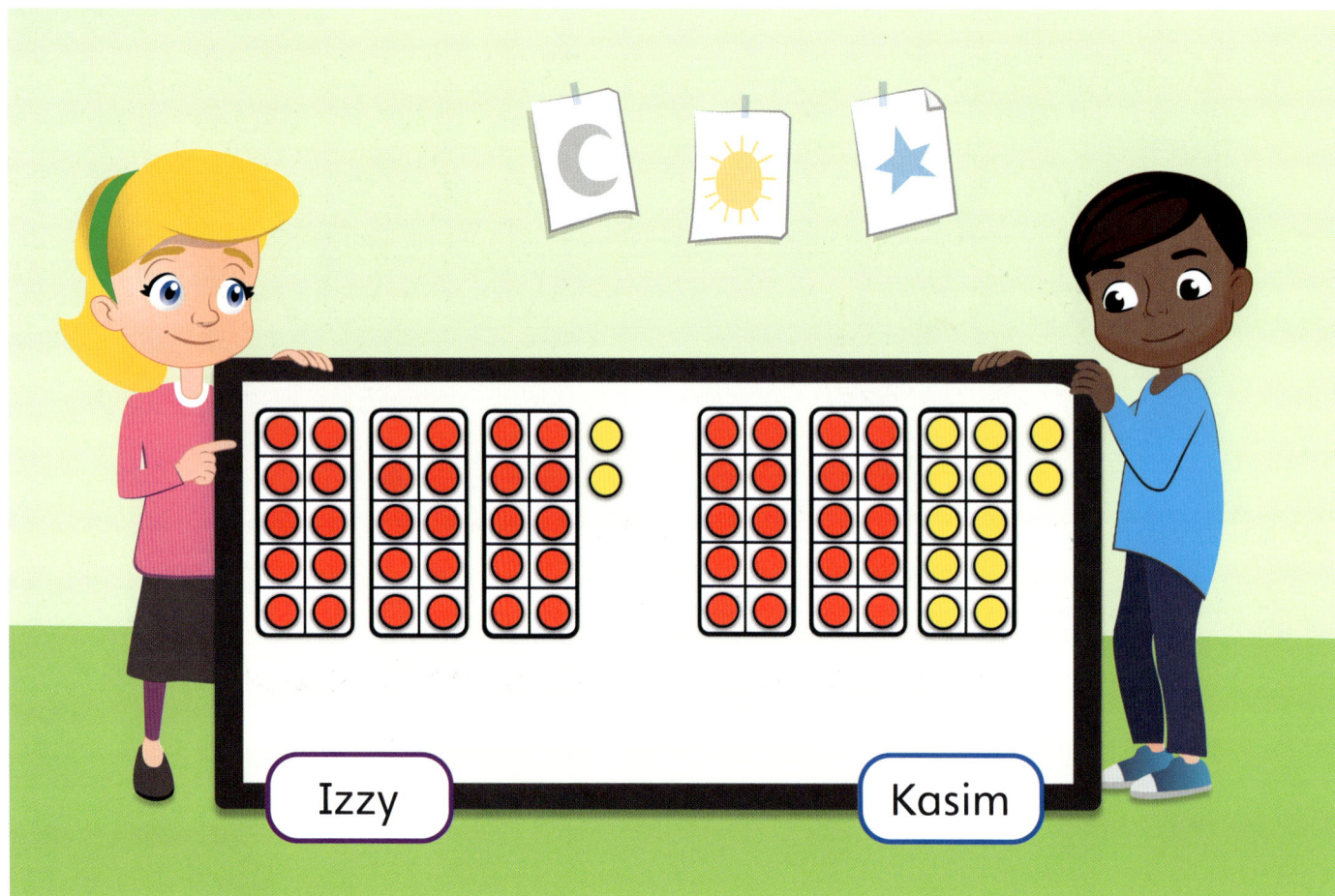

1 **a)** What number has Izzy made?

What number has Kasim made?

What is the same and what is different about their representations?

b) Draw a part-whole model for each child's representation.

Share

a) Each ten frame has 10 counters

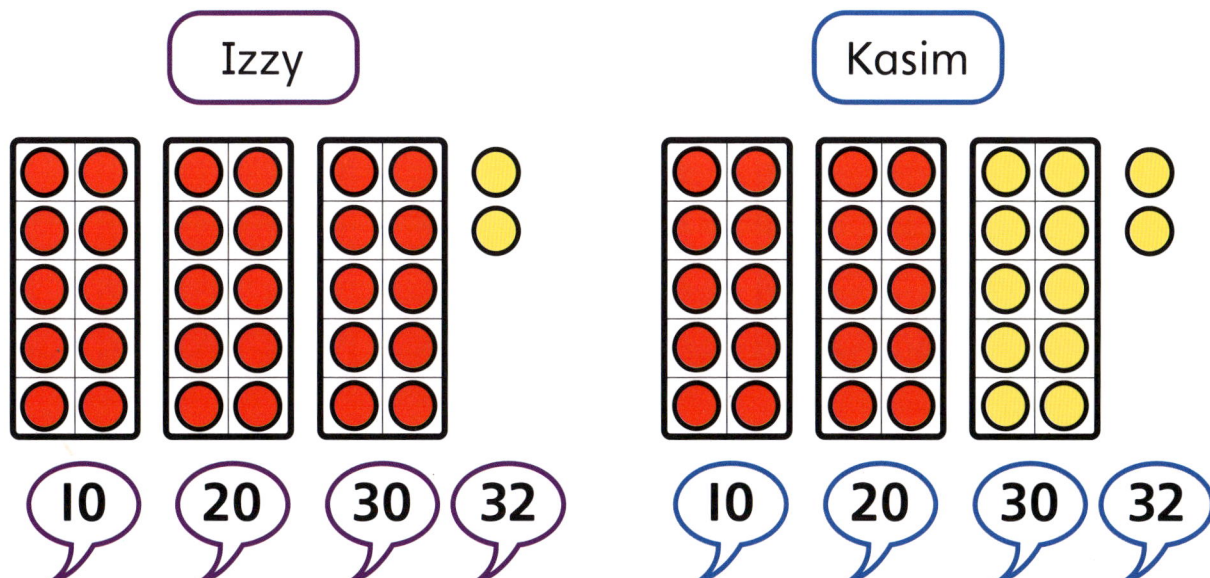

Izzy

Kasim

10   20   30   32   10   20   30   32

Izzy and Kasim have both made the number 32.

They both have 3 tens and 2 ones.

They have used different amounts of each colour counter.

b)

Izzy

Kasim

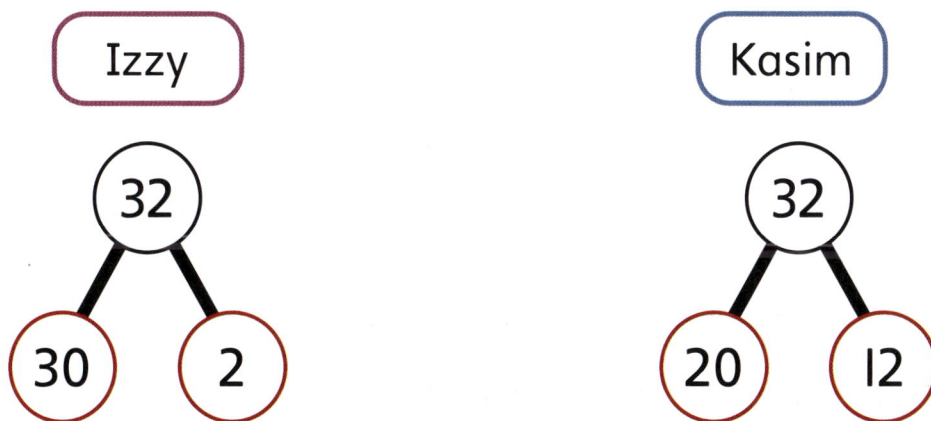

I can see that 32 can be partitioned in different ways.

37

Think together

1. Complete the part-whole models.

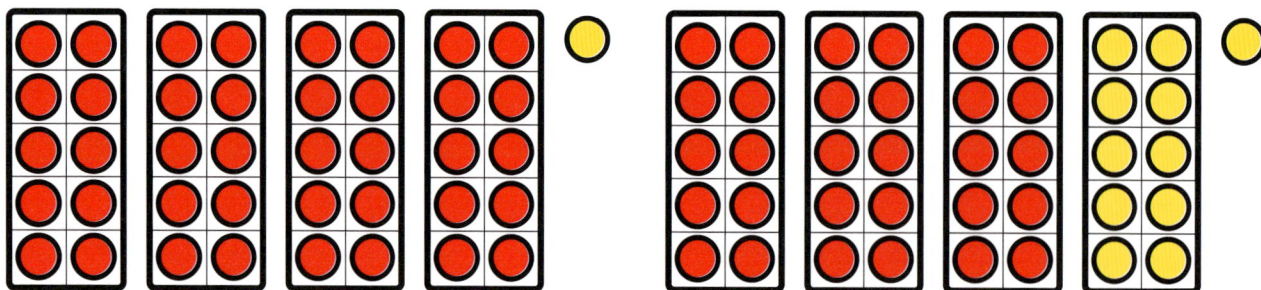

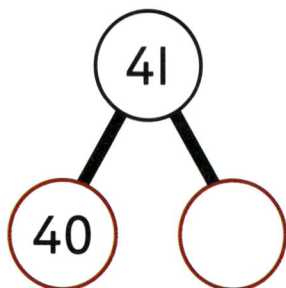

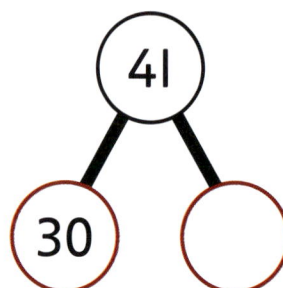

```
      41                          41
     /  \                        /  \
   40    ( )                   30    ( )
```

2. Complete the part-whole models.

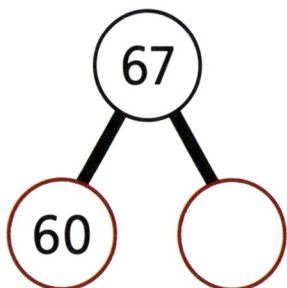

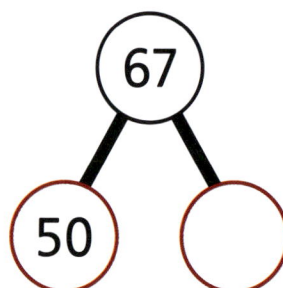

```
      67                          67
     /  \                        /  \
   60    ( )                   50    ( )
```

I used base 10 equipment to help me.

3 Max has made 75 in 10s and 1s.

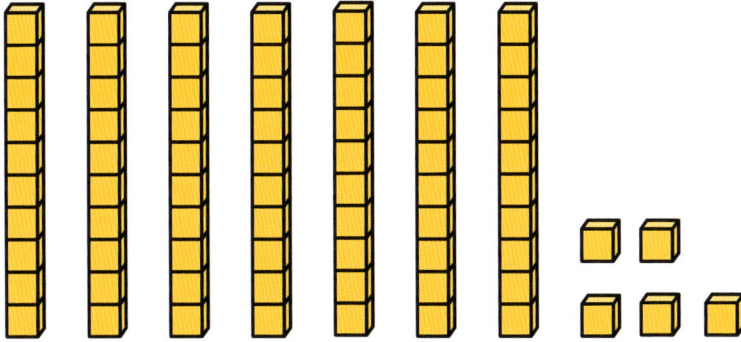

He uses it to partition this number.

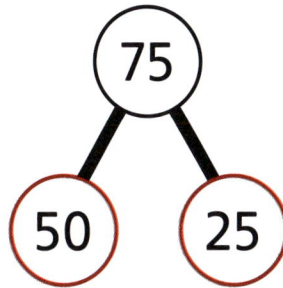

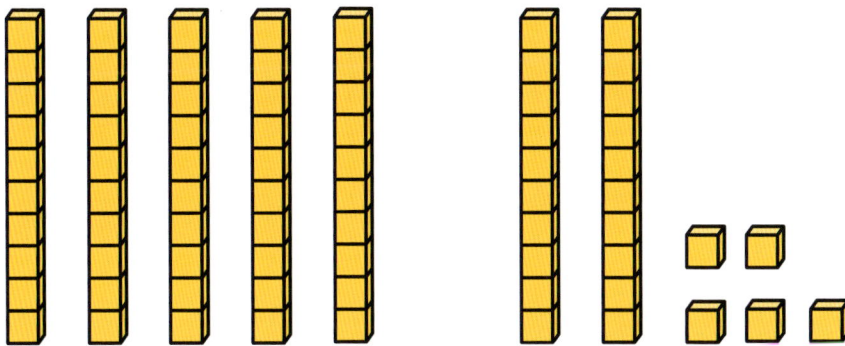

How many ways can you partition 75?

I wonder if there is a way I can do this without missing any.

→ Practice book 2A p27

Write numbers to 100 in expanded form

Discover

1   a) What is the value of the  and the ?

   b) What is the value of the ?

Share

I made the numbers out of base 10 equipment to help me.

a)

$$35 = 30 + 5$$

So △ = 5

$$54 = 50 + 4$$

So ● = 50

b)

$$28 = 20 + 8$$

So ★ = 28

Think together

1　Find the missing numbers.

a)　$10 + 5 = \boxed{}$

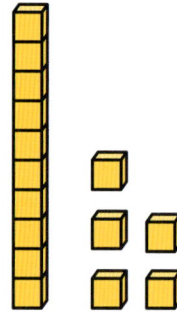

b)　$63 = 60 + \boxed{}$

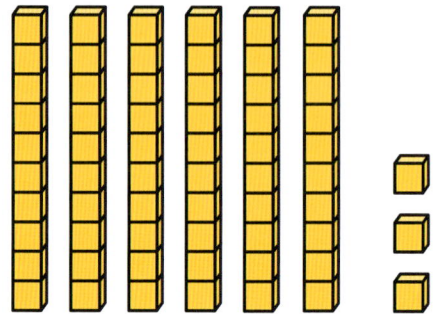

c)　$27 = \boxed{} + 7$

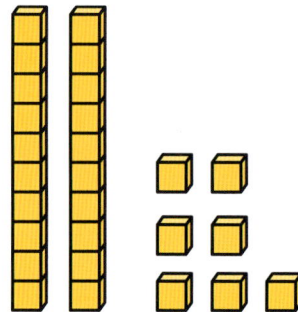

2　Complete the number sentences.

a)　$46 = \boxed{} + \boxed{}$

c)　$\boxed{} = 60 + 1$

b)　$53 = \boxed{} + \boxed{}$

d)　$70 + 3 = \boxed{}$

CHALLENGE

3 Here is the number 52.

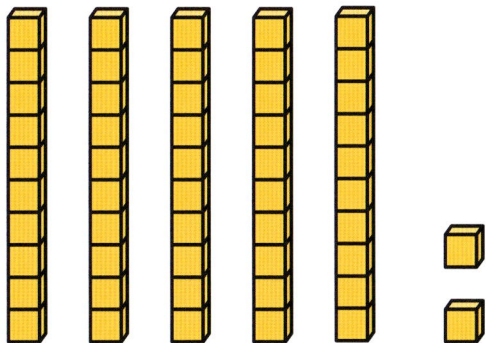

Use 10s and 1s to work out the missing numbers.

52 = 50 + ☐

52 = 40 + ☐

52 = 30 + ☐

52 = 20 + ☐

This feels like the work we did when partitioning numbers.

→ Practice book 2A p30

10s on a number line to 100

Discover

Myra

1 a) Will Myra have room to carry on her number line to 100?

   b) How could Myra draw a number line from 0 to 100 which does not take up as much space?

Share

a)

Myra's number line goes up in 1s.

I can see that Myra cannot fit her number line up to 100 on the card.

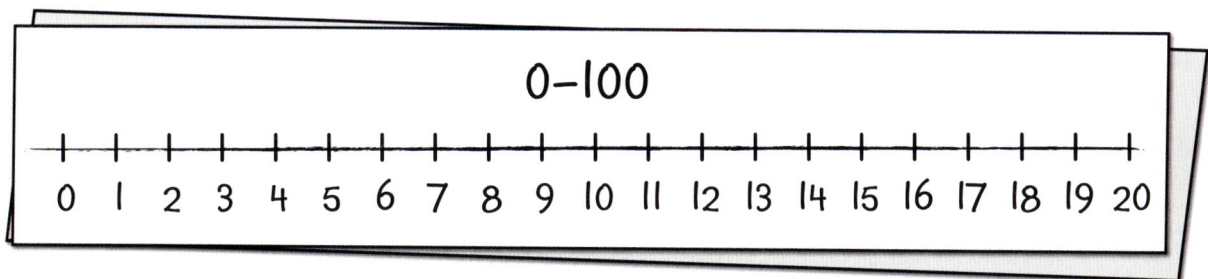

0–100

0 1 2 3 4 5 6 7 8 9 10 11 12 13 14 15 16 17 18 19 20

b) Some number lines go up in 10s instead of 1s.

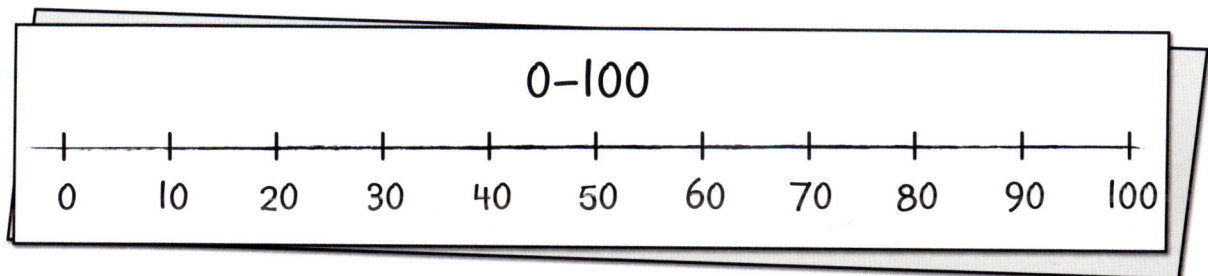

0–100

0 10 20 30 40 50 60 70 80 90 100

We know where the other numbers go, but do not always need to label them all.

Think together

1 What numbers are shown by the arrows?

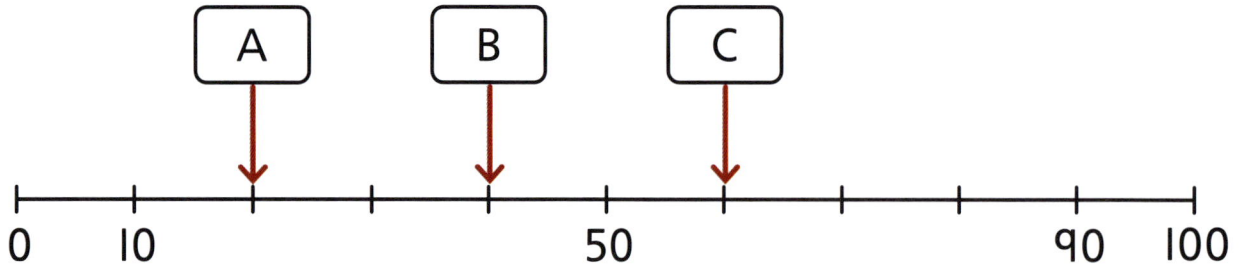

A   B   C

0   10   50   90   100

2 Point to where each number should be on the number line.

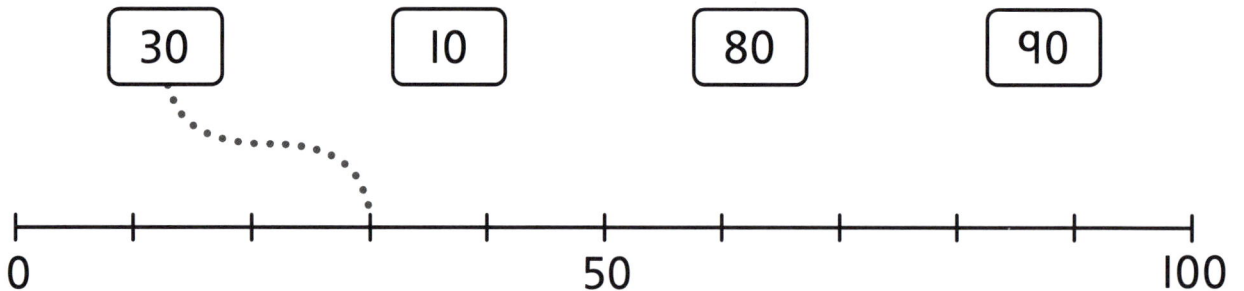

30   10   80   90

0   50   100

I will count up in 10s.

3 **a)** Compare these number lines.

What do you notice?

CHALLENGE

```
0  1  2  3  4  5  6  7  8  9  10
```

```
0  10  20  30  40  50  60  70  80  90  100
```

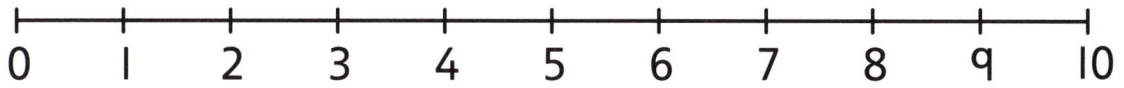

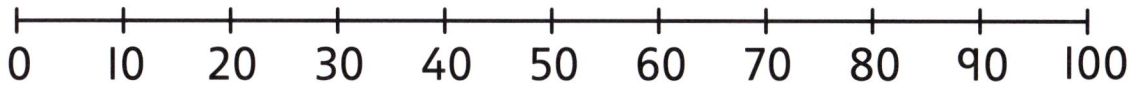

I think the first one goes up in 1s, the other in 10s.

b) Here is another number line.

Compare it with the number lines above.

What is the same?

What is different?

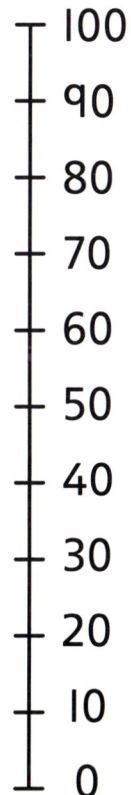

This is a vertical number line. I wonder where I might see one.

```
100
90
80
70
60
50
40
30
20
10
0
```

47

→ Practice book 2A p33

10s and 1s on a number line to 100

Discover

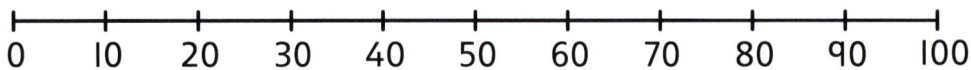

Draw a number line from 0–100

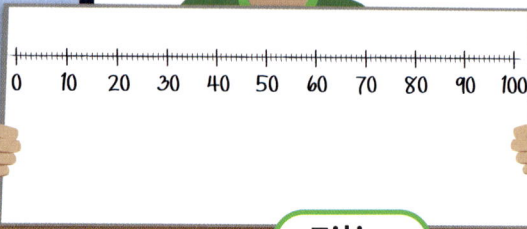
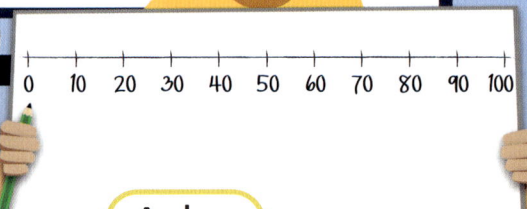

Filip

Asha

Filip

Asha

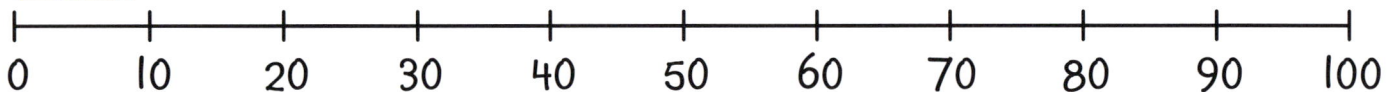

1 **a)** What is the same and what is different about Filip's and Asha's number lines?

b) Where would Filip put 34 on his number line?

Share

a) Asha's number line goes up in 10s.

Filip's goes up in 10s and 1s.

They both go from 0 to 100.

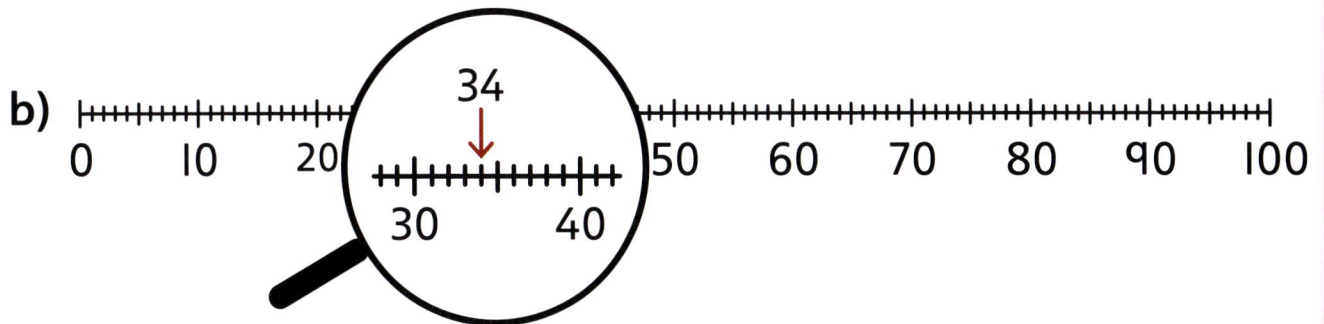

b)

The 4th mark after 30 shows 34.

I counted in 1s
from 30 to 40.

Think together

1 Say the missing numbers.

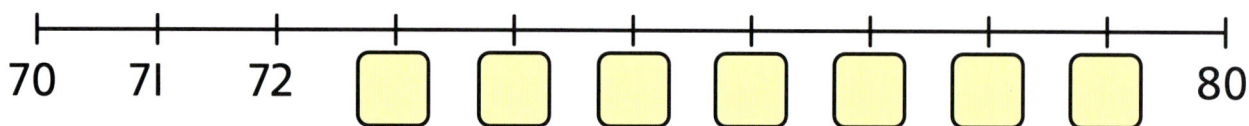

70   71   72   ☐   ☐   ☐   ☐   ☐   ☐   ☐   80

2 What number is this?

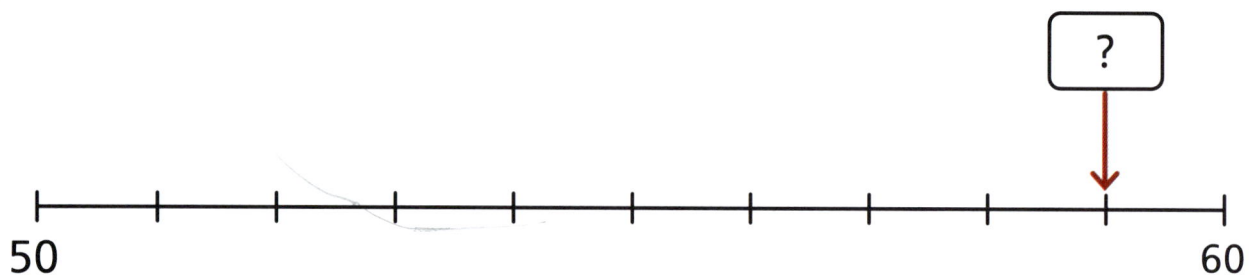

?

50   60

I will count on from 50.

I think it is easier to count back.

3 Trace a line with your finger to match each number to the number line.

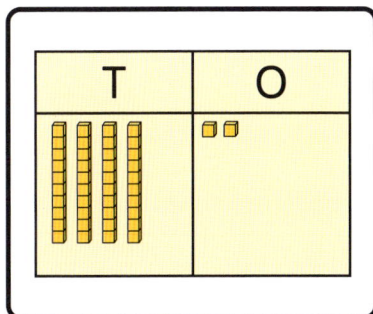

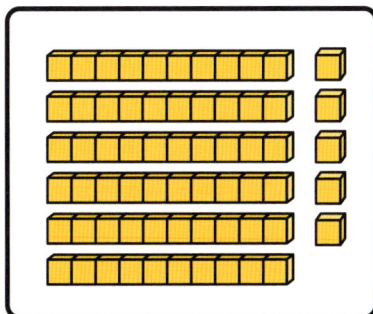

CHALLENGE

T	O

89

```
|++++++++++|++++++++++|++++++++++|++++++++++|++++++++++|++++++++++|++++++++++|++++++++++|++++++++++|++++++++++|
0        10        20        30        40        50        60        70        80        90       100
```

I will look at the 10s first, then the 1s.

51

→ Practice book 2A p36

Estimate numbers on a number line

Discover

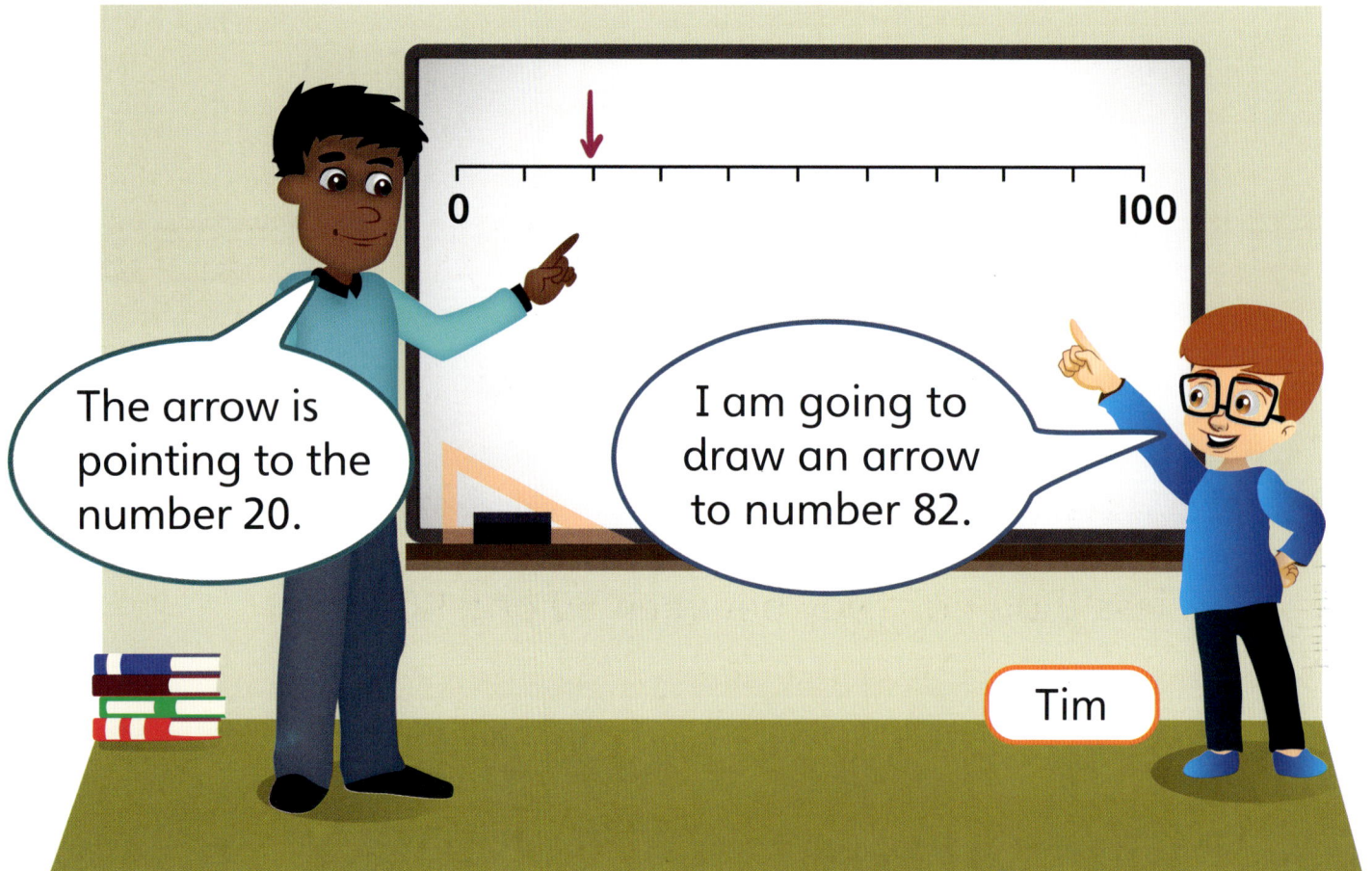

The arrow is pointing to the number 20.

I am going to draw an arrow to number 82.

Tim

1 **a)** Is the teacher correct?

b) Where will Tim's arrow go?

Share

a)

I checked by writing in all the numbers.

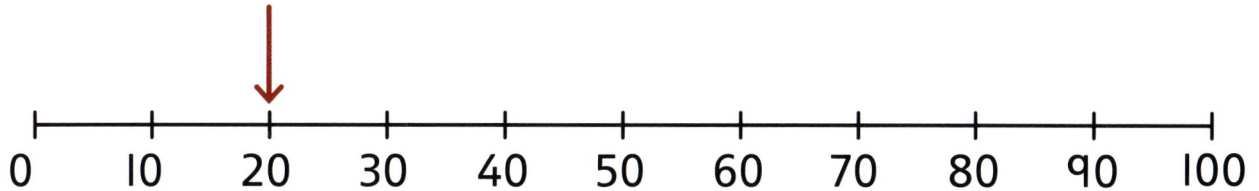

The teacher is correct. The arrow is pointing to 20.

b) 82 lies between 80 and 90.

It is less than half-way between 80 and 90.

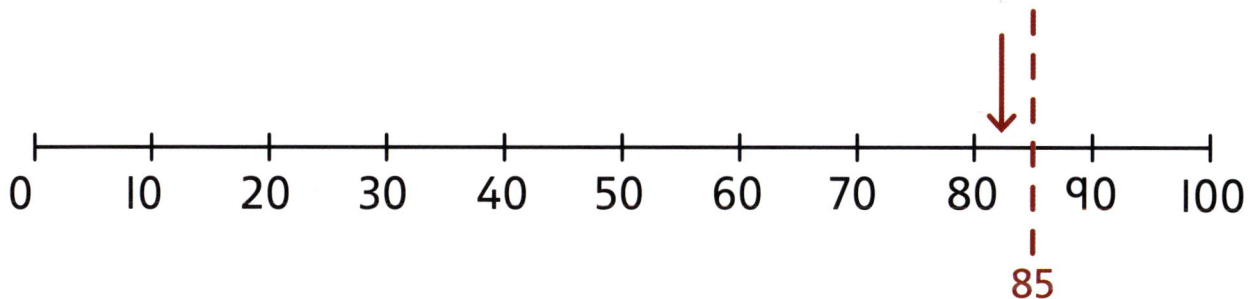

85

The answer is only an estimate. It might not be exact.

Think together

1 **a)** What numbers are the arrows pointing to?

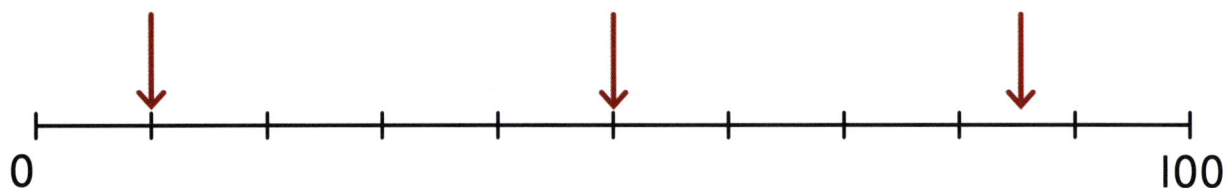

b) Estimate where you think 99 will go on the number line. Point to it.

2 Point to where 67 is on each number line.

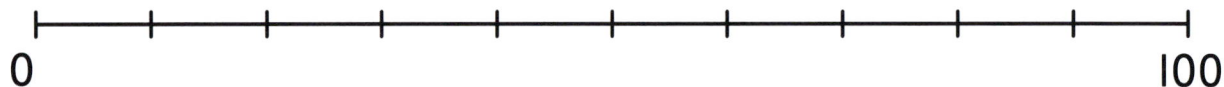

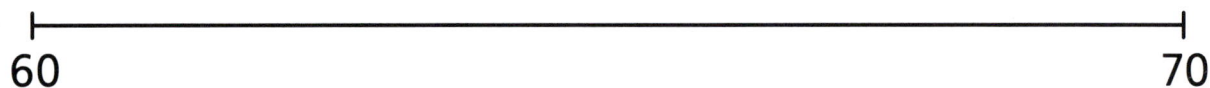

3 Look at the number line from 0 to 100.

Where should each number go on the number line?

CHALLENGE

| 50 | 80 | 2 |

0 ——————————————————————————— 100

First, I am going to work out where 50 goes.

I am going to copy the number line to help me.

→ Practice book 2A p39

Compare numbers ❶

Discover

Matt

Anna

❶ a) How many cookies does each child have?

b) Who has the fewest cookies?

Share

a) and **b)**

I counted the 10s and then the 1s.

Matt		Anna

10 20 30 40 43

10 20 30 40 50

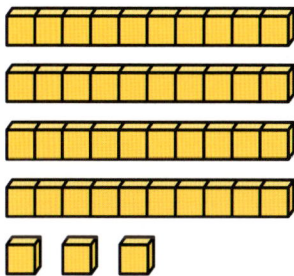

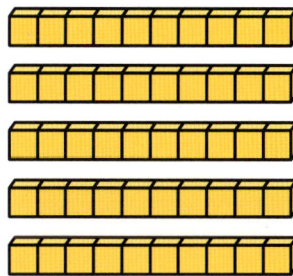

Matt has fewer cookies than Anna.

Anna has more cookies than Matt.

I used base 10 equipment to represent the cookies.

Think together

1 Copy and complete the number sentences.

a)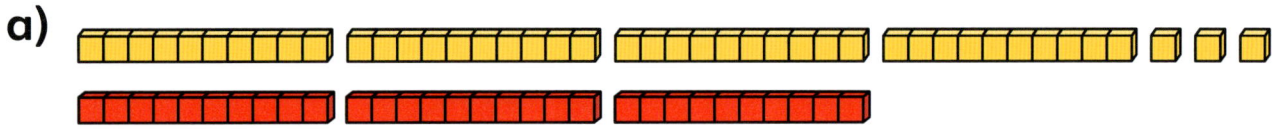

☐ is less than ☐.

b)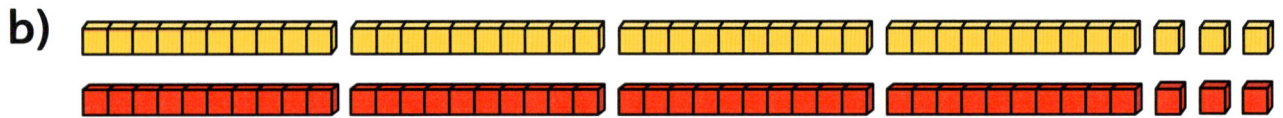

☐ is _____ ☐.

2 Who has more cubes?

Ros   Tim

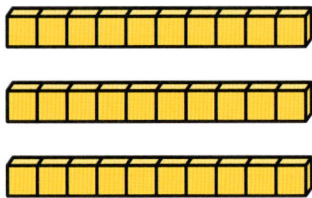   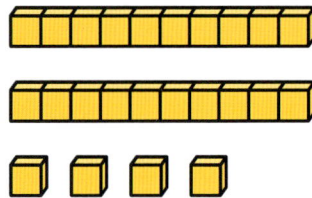

I put the 10s rods and and 1s cubes in lines.

3 **a)** There are 10 straws in each bundle.

How many straws does each person have?

Mo

Jan

b) Point to these numbers on the number line.

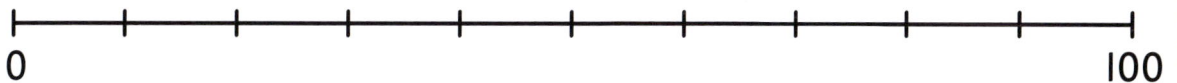

0   100

c) Who has fewer straws? Who has more straws?

I will use the number line to help me.

59

→ Practice book 2A p42

Compare numbers 2

Discover

Asif

Beth

I have 43 leaves.

I have 57 leaves.

1 **a)** Who has more leaves?

b) Copy and complete the number sentence using <, > or =.

43 ◯ 57

Share

a)

Asif   Beth

T	O
4	3

T	O
5	7

Beth's number has more 10s than Asif's.

Beth has more leaves than Asif.

b) 43 has fewer 10s than 57.

So 43 < 57.

You can also write 57 > 43.

> < means less than or smaller than
> > means more than or greater than

If the numbers are equal, we use = .

Think together

1 **a)** Which number is greater?

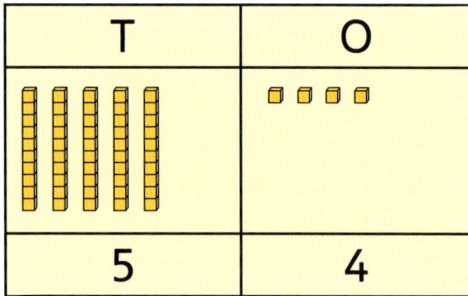

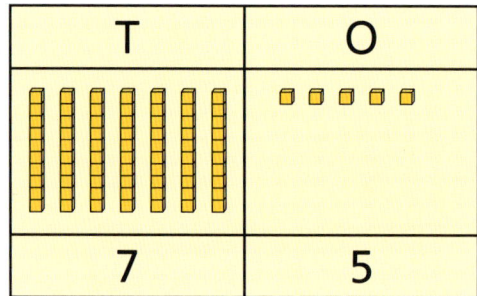

T	O
5	4

T	O
7	5

b) Complete the number sentence using <, > or =.

54 ◯ 75

2 Which number is smaller?

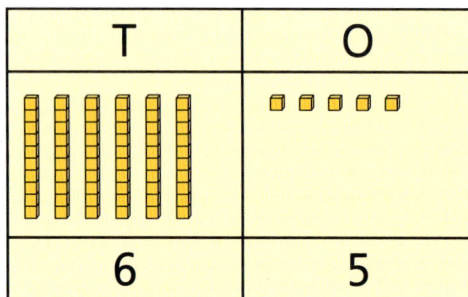

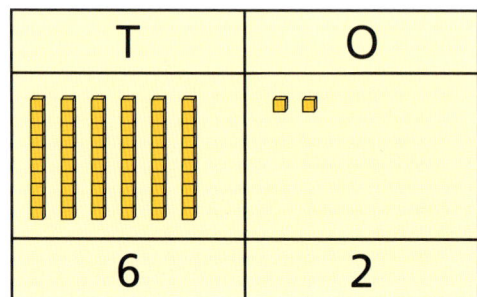

T	O
6	5

T	O
6	2

I can see the 10s are the same and I can compare the 1s.

③ Use <, > or = to compare the numbers.

CHALLENGE

a)

T	O
6	4

◯

T	O
2	6

b)

T	O
5	7

◯

T	O
7	0

c)   57 ◯ 54

I can tell which is greater just by looking at the 10s.

I wonder if that always works.

63

→ Practice book 2A p45

Order numbers

Discover

Sunflower	Height
Dan's	33
Eva's	45
Felix's	38

1 **a)** Whose sunflower is the tallest?

b) Whose sunflower is shortest?

64

Share

I compared the 10s and 1s.

I made the numbers using base 10 equipment.

a)

Felix's	
T	O
3	8

Dan's	
T	O
3	3

Eva's	
T	O
4	5

45 has the most 10s, so it is the greatest number.

The tallest sunflower, C, is Eva's.

b) 38 and 33 both have 3 tens.

Dan's has fewer 1s than Felix's

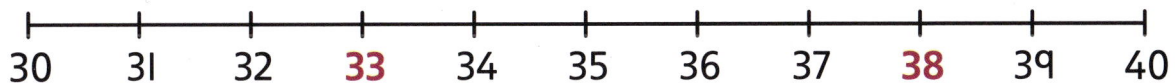

```
30   31   32   33   34   35   36   37   38   39   40
```

33 < 38

So Dan's sunflower, B, is the shortest.

I used a number line to help me see which number was greater.

Think together

1 Sort from greatest to smallest.
Sort from smallest to greatest.

67

31

63

Greatest   Smallest

☐ > ☐ > ☐

Smallest   Greatest

☐ < ☐ < ☐

2 Choose numbers to complete these statements.

30 < ☐ < 40

65 > ☐ > 55

100 > ☐ > ☐ > 0

3   Play guess the mystery number.

CHALLENGE

Is it 80?

Your guess is too big.

Is it 10?

Your guess is too small.

So it must be between…

Reena

Ms Falana

```
|-----|-----|--------------------------------|-----|
0    10                                  80    100
```

Discuss with a partner a good way to work out the number.

Is 99 a good guess?

I guess 1, then 2, then 3, then 4 … all the way up to 100.

67

→ Practice book 2A p48

Count in 2s, 5s and 10s

Discover

It is easier to count you all if you line up in pairs.

1 **a)** Count the children onto the bus in pairs.

b) Count the fingers and thumbs of 6 of the children.

Share

a)

2   4   6   8   10   12

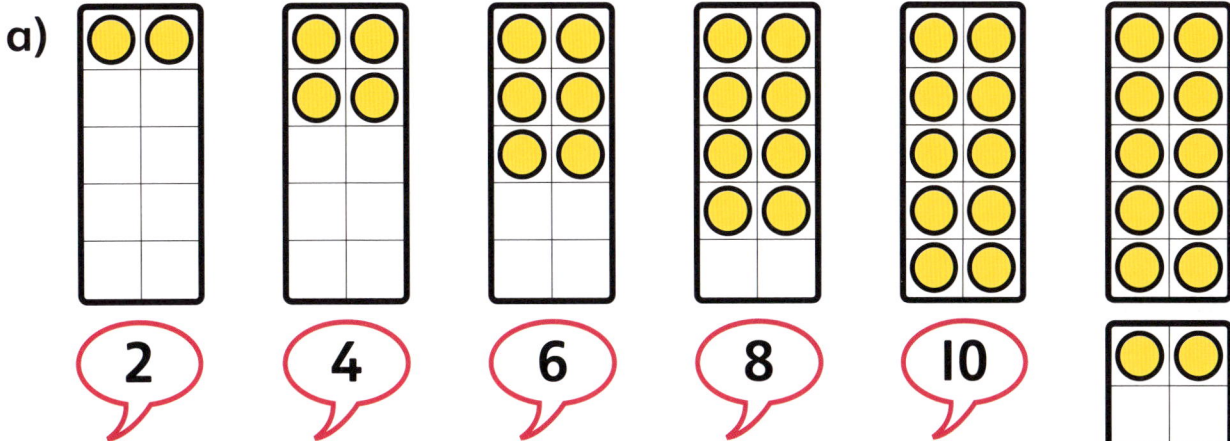

I counted them all in 2s.

b)

0 5 10 15 20 25 30 35 40 45 50 55 60

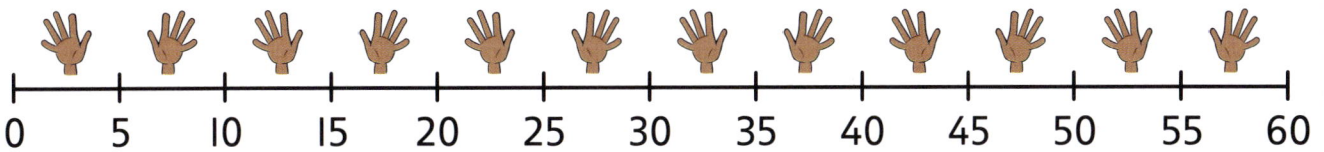

I counted in 5s.

I could have counted in 10s.

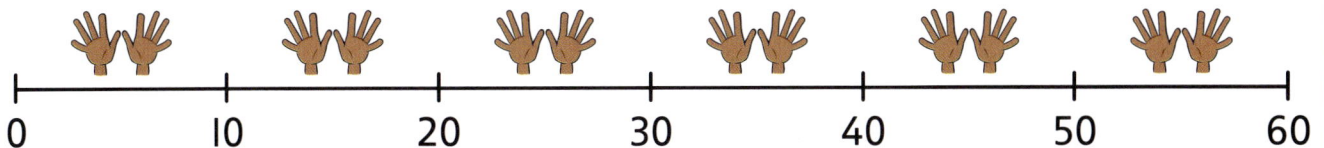

0   10   20   30   40   50   60

Think together

1 Continue the counts to at least 50.

a) 0   5   10   15   20

b) 0   10   20

c) 0   2   4   6

I wonder what I am counting in each time.

2 Copy and complete these counts.

a)

34	36		40			

b)

45	50	55			

c) 100, 90, ☐, 70, ☐, ☐

3 Copy and complete the number cards.

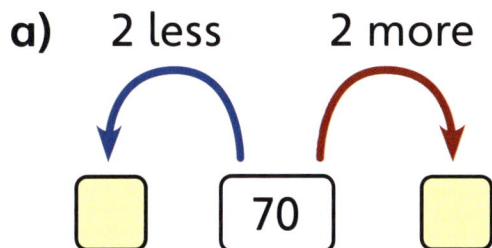

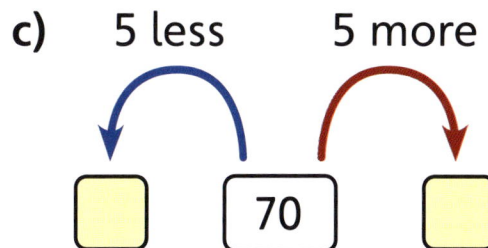

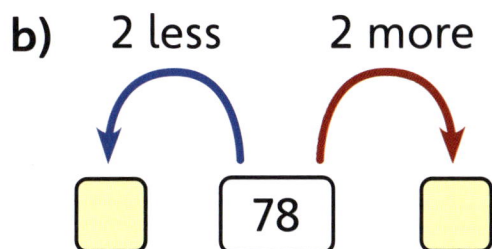

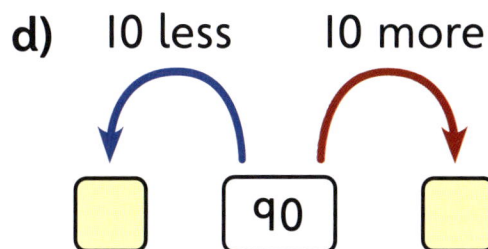

CHALLENGE

a) 2 less   2 more

☐   70   ☐

c) 5 less   5 more

☐   70   ☐

b) 2 less   2 more

☐   78   ☐

d) 10 less   10 more

☐   90   ☐

I will count in 2s, 5s or 10s to check my answers.

71

→ Practice book 2A p51

Counts in 3s

Discover

I made this pattern using sticks.

1 **a)** How many sticks did Andy use?

b) Andy wants to add another row of triangles at the bottom.

How many more sticks does he need?

Share

I will count the sticks one by one.

I will count in 3s.

a)

| 1 | 2 | **3** | 4 | 5 | **6** | 7 | 8 | **9** | 10 | 11 | **12** | 13 | 14 | **15** | 16 | 17 | **18** |

0 1 2 **3** 4 5 **6** 7 8 **9** 10 11 **12** 13 14 **15** 16 17 **18**

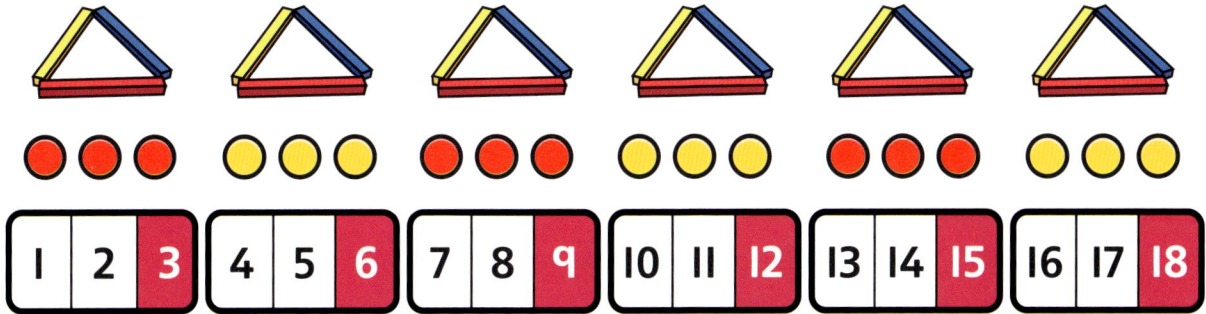

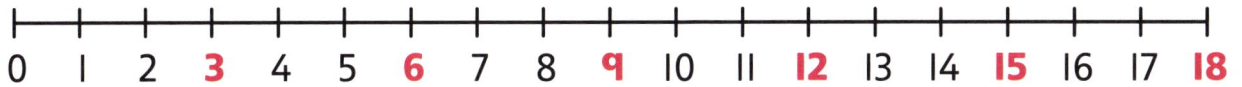

Andy used 18 sticks.

b) There are 4 triangles in the new row.

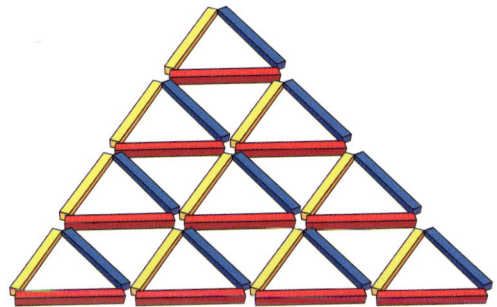

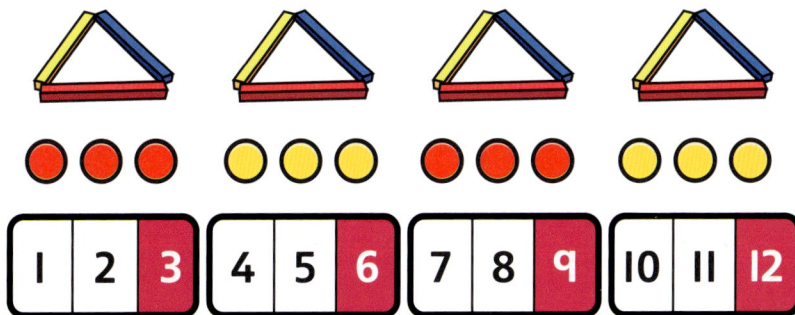

| 1 | 2 | **3** | 4 | 5 | **6** | 7 | 8 | **9** | 10 | 11 | **12** |

Andy needs 12 more sticks.

Think together

Count in 3s.

1 **a)** How many trees are there?

1	2		4	5		7	8		10	11	

b) How many birds are there?

1	2		4	5		7	8		10	11		13	14	

2 The base of Steve's castle has 12 blocks.

How many blocks did Steve use altogether?

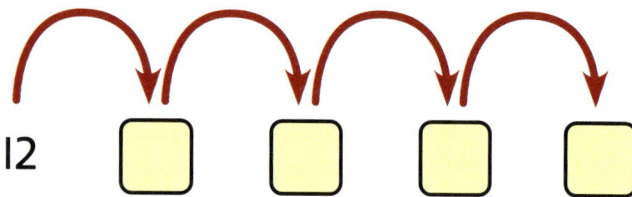

12

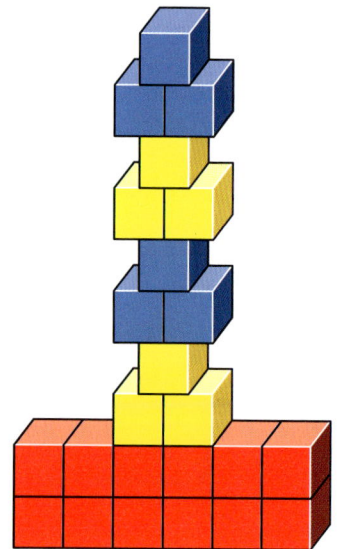

CHALLENGE

3 Jake counts up in 2s from 2.

2	4					

Zara counts up in 3s from 3.

3	6					

Which numbers do Jake and Zara both write?

I will work out which numbers they will both write up to 30.

75

→ Practice book 2A p54

End of unit check

Your teacher will ask you these questions.

1 How many counters?

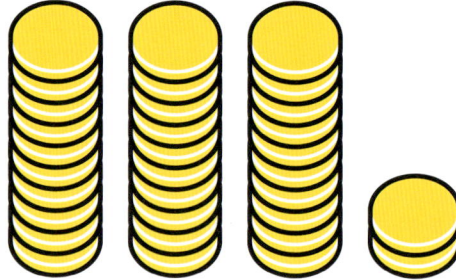

A 23   B 32   C 4   D 40

2 What is shown?

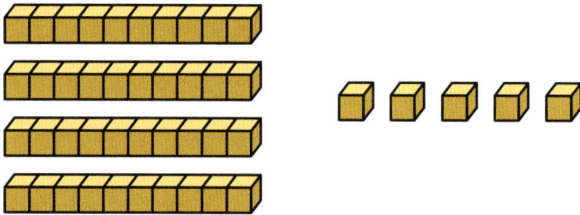

A 4 tens and 5 ones is 45   C 4 ones and 4 tens is 44

B 5 tens and 4 ones is 54   D 5 ones and 4 tens is 54

3 Which part-whole model does not show 41?

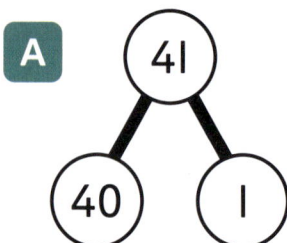

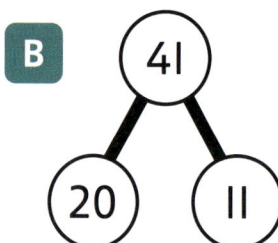

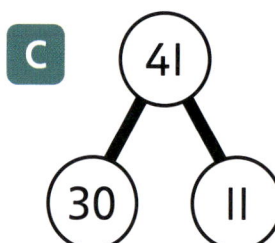

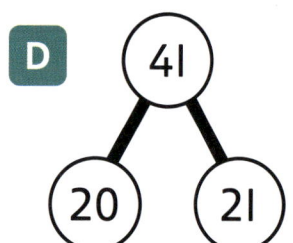

A 41 / 40 1

B 41 / 20 11

C 41 / 30 11

D 41 / 20 21

4 Which number could go in the box?

◻ is greater than 55 but less than 63.

A 65   **B** 55   **C** 60   **D** 64

5 What number is the arrow pointing to?

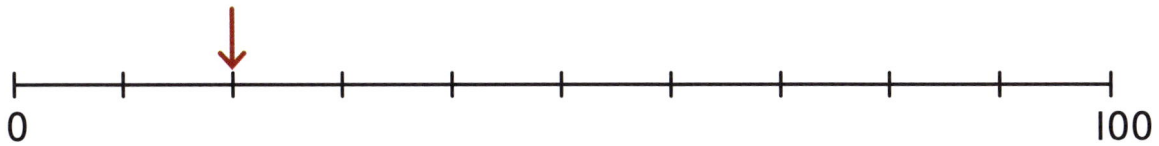

0 ——————————————————— 100

A 2   **B** 10   **C** 12   **D** 20

Think!

Which diagram shows a different number? Prove it.

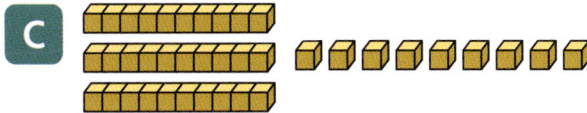

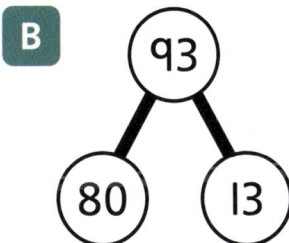

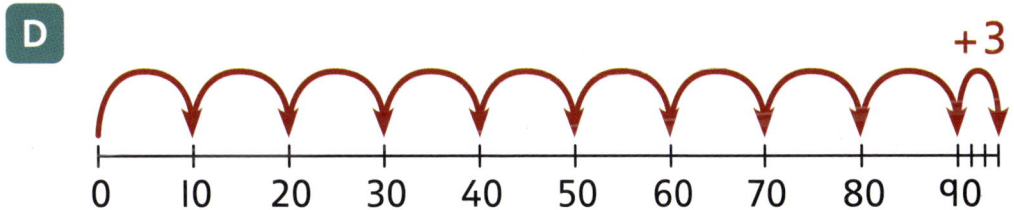

A | 9 | 3 |

C

B 93 / 80 \ 13

D +3

0 10 20 30 40 50 60 70 80 90

These words will help you.

tens   part whole

ones   number line

→ Practice book 2A p57

Unit 2
Addition and subtraction ①

In this unit we will …

⚡ Use related number facts
⚡ Compare number sentences
⚡ Make number bonds to 100
⚡ Add and subtract 1s and 10s
⚡ Add a 2-digit and a 1-digit number
⚡ Subtract a 1-digit number from a 2-digit number

We have used this before. What is the same? What is different?

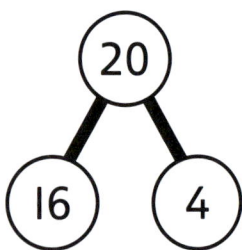

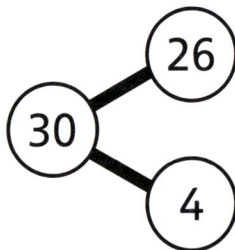

20
16 4

30 26
4

We need some maths words. Are any of these new?

add   subtract   difference   sum

fact family   number sentence   total

number bonds   multiples   plus   minus

How many pencils are there altogether? You can use a ten frame and counters to find the total.

10

10

Fact families

Discover

1 **a)** What does each number in the part-whole model represent?

b) Copy and complete the fact family.

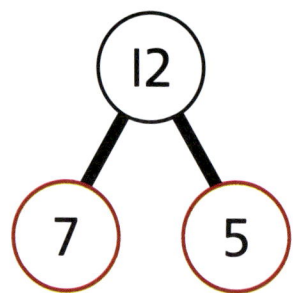

□ + □ = □   □ − □ = □

□ + □ = □   □ − □ = □

12
7   5

Share

a)

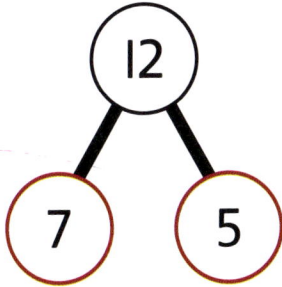

The number 7 represents apples in the tree.

The number 5 represents apples on the ground.

The number 12 represents the total number of apples.

part + part = whole
whole − part = part

b) These four facts make up a fact family.

$7 + 5 = 12$

$5 + 7 = 12$

$12 − 5 = 7$

$12 − 7 = 5$

We can add the parts in any order. We always get the same total.

I started with the whole and took away a part.

Think together

1 Complete the fact family for the part-whole model.

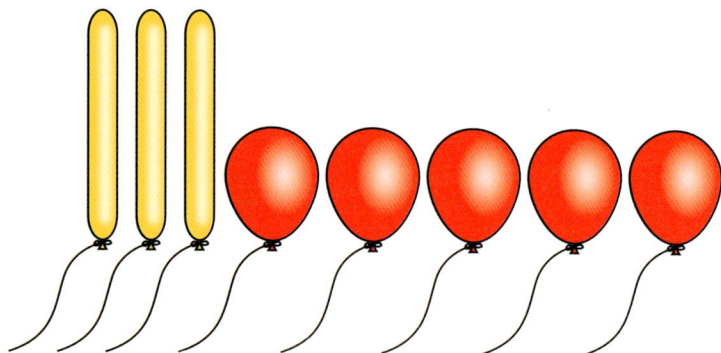

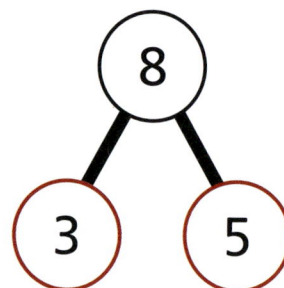

$$\Box + \Box = \Box \qquad \Box - \Box = \Box$$

$$\Box + \Box = \Box \qquad \Box - \Box = \Box$$

2 Look at the bar model.

16	
10	6

a) Which of these additions is correct?

$10 + 6 = 16$

$16 + 6 = 10$

b) Which of these subtractions is correct?

$6 - 16 = 10$

$16 - 10 = 6$

CHALLENGE

3 Meg writes down a number bond.

$$3 + 4 = 7$$

a) Complete the part-whole model for the bond.

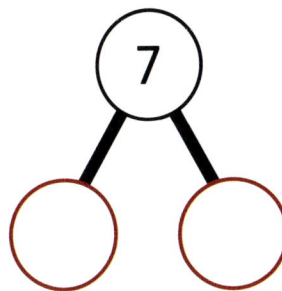

7

b) Write down the fact family for the part-whole model.

I can work out other facts using one I am given.

I think I can write down 8 facts. I remember doing these last year.

83

→ Practice book 2A p59

Learn number bonds

Discover

+	0	1	2	3	4	5	6	7	8	9	10
0	0+0	0+1	0+2	0+3	0+4	0+5	0+6	0+7	0+8	0+9	0+10
1	1+0	1+1	1+2	1+3	1+4	1+5	1+6	1+7	1+8	1+9	
2	2+0	2+1	2+2	2+3	2+4	2+5	2+6	2+7	2+8		
3	3+0	3+1	3+2	3+3	3+4	3+5	3+6	3+7			
4	4+0	4+1	4+2	4+3	4+4	4+5	4+6				
5	5+0	5+1	5+2	5+3	5+4	5+5					
6	6+0	6+1	6+2	6+3	6+4						
7	7+0	7+1	7+2	7+3							
8	8+0	8+1	8+2								
9	9+0	9+1									
10	10+0										

I'm going to work out what happens when you add 1.

I'm going to work out what happens when you add zero.

Gita

Zac

1 **a)** Help Gita to work out what happens when you add zero.

b) Help Zac to work out what happens when you add 1.

Share

a) When you add zero, the number does not change.

$1 + 0 = 1$ $0 + 1 = 1$

$2 + 0 = 2$ $0 + 2 = 2$

$3 + 0 = 3$ $0 + 3 = 3$

You can add two numbers in any order.

b)

I used my counting skills.

When you add 1, count to the next number.

1	2	3	4	5	6	7	8	9	10

$2 + 1 = 3$ $8 + 1 = 9$

$1 + 2 = 3$ $1 + 8 = 9$

Think together

① Find all the number bonds to 10.

+	0	1	2	3	4	5	6	7	8	9	10
0	0+0	0+1	0+2	0+3	0+4	0+5	0+6	0+7	0+8	0+9	0+10
1	1+0	1+1	1+2	1+3	1+4	1+5	1+6	1+7	1+8	1+9	
2	2+0	2+1	2+2	2+3	2+4	2+5	2+6	2+7	2+8		
3	3+0	3+1	3+2	3+3	3+4	3+5	3+6	3+7			
4	4+0	4+1	4+2	4+3	4+4	4+5	4+6				
5	5+0	5+1	5+2	5+3	5+4	5+5					
6	6+0	6+1	6+2	6+3	6+4						
7	7+0	7+1	7+2	7+3							
8	8+0	8+1	8+2								
9	9+0	9+1									
10	10+0										

② Use number bonds to complete the number sentences.

$2 + 2 =$ ☐ $4 - 2 =$ ☐

$3 + 3 =$ ☐ $6 - 3 =$ ☐

$4 + 4 =$ ☐ $8 - 4 =$ ☐

I wonder where these are on the grid.

CHALLENGE

3 **a)** Discuss a good method to work out the highlighted facts.

+	0	1	2	3	4	5	6	7	8	9	10
0	0+0	0+1	0+2	0+3	0+4	0+5	0+6	0+7	0+8	0+9	0+10
1	1+0	1+1	1+2	1+3	1+4	1+5	1+6	1+7	1+8	1+9	
2	2+0	2+1	2+2	2+3	2+4	2+5	2+6	2+7	2+8		
3	3+0	3+1	3+2	3+3	3+4	3+5	3+6	3+7			
4	4+0	4+1	4+2	4+3	4+4	4+5	4+6				
5	5+0	5+1	5+2	5+3	5+4	5+5					
6	6+0	6+1	6+2	6+3	6+4						
7	7+0	7+1	7+2	7+3							
8	8+0	8+1	8+2								
9	9+0	9+1									
10	10+0										

> I will count on 2 more to add 2.

b) How many facts in the table do you know off by heart?

> I will learn as many of these number bonds as possible off by heart.

→ Practice book 2A p62

Add and subtract two multiples of 10

Discover

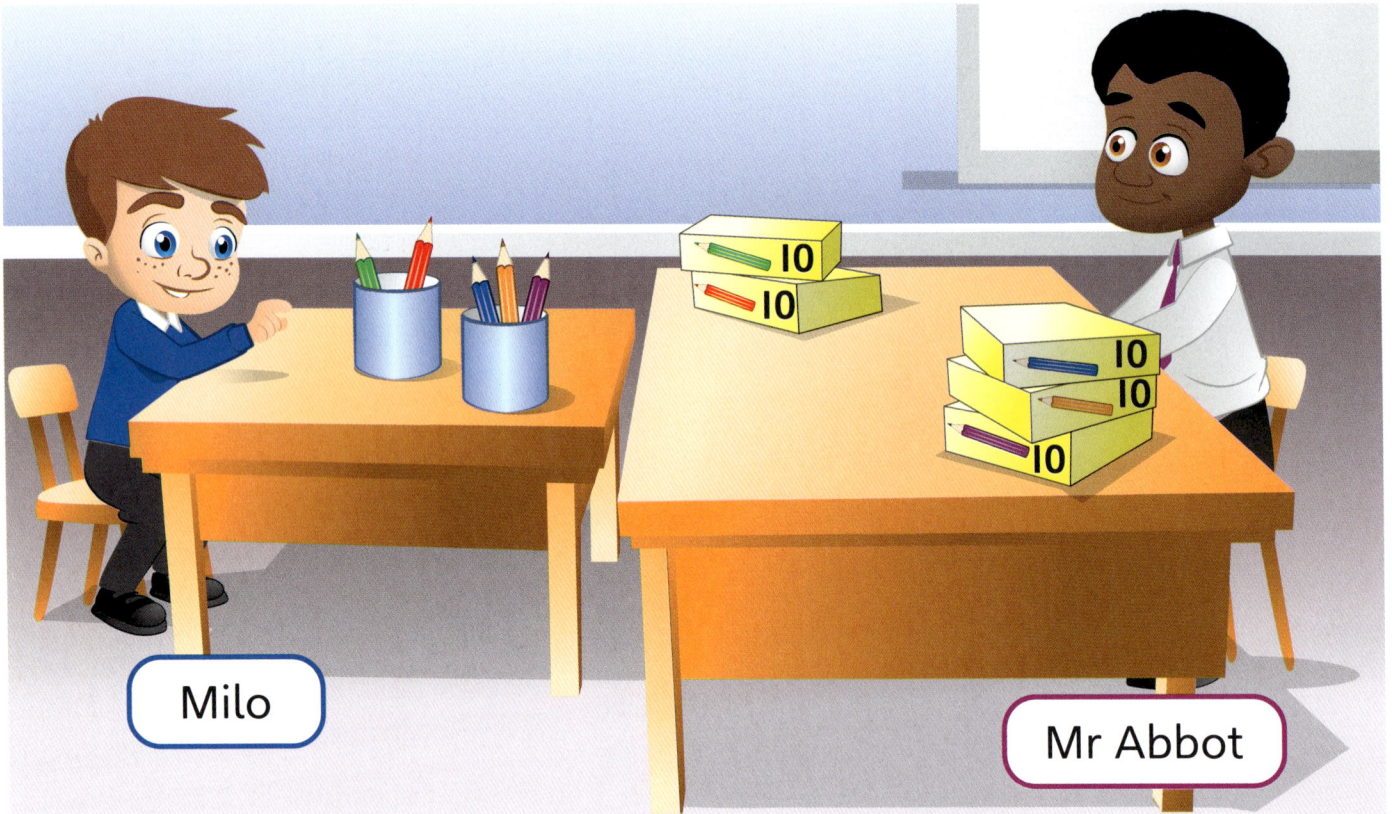

Milo

Mr Abbot

1 **a)** How many pencils does Milo have?

b) How many pencils does Mr Abbot have?

Share

a)

 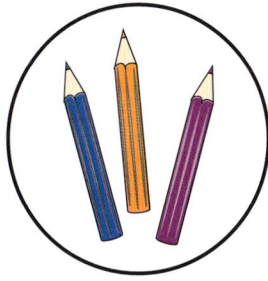 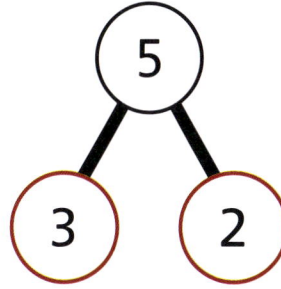

2 ones   +   3 ones   =   5 ones

2 + 3 = 5

Milo has 5 pencils.

I wrote
5 = 2 + 3.

b)

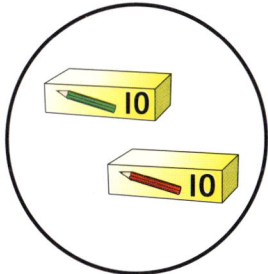   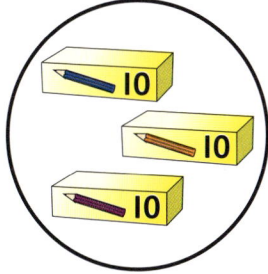

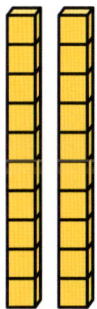   +   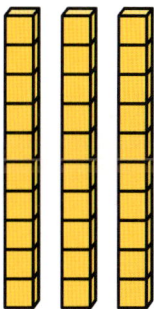   =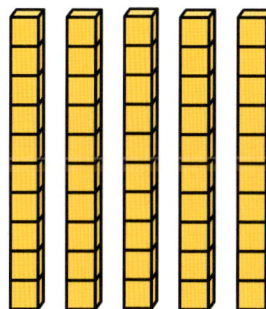

2 tens   +   3 tens   =   5 tens

20 + 30 = 50

Mr Abbot has 50 pencils.

Think together

1 **a)** Complete the following.

 +  = ☐ pencils

 +  = ☐ apples

4 ones + 3 ones = ☐ ones

4 tens + 3 tens = ☐ tens

b) Complete the following.

4 + 3 = ☐

40 + 30 = ☐

2 Use the part-whole model to complete the number sentences.

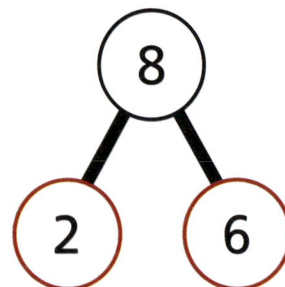

2 + 6 = ☐

20 + 60 = ☐

CHALLENGE

3 Here is a number bond.

$$5 + 1 = 6$$

Complete the number sentences.

$50 + 10 = \boxed{}$

$10 + \boxed{} = 60$

$60 - 50 = \boxed{}$

$10 = \boxed{} - 50$

I will use the number sentence 5 + 1 = 6 to get the answers.

I will use base 10 equipment to help.

91

→ Practice book 2A p65

Complements to 100 (tens)

Discover

1 **a)** How many beads are there altogether?

b) Complete the number sentence.

$60 + \boxed{} = 100$

Share

a) There are 10 beads in a row.

There are 10 rows of beads.

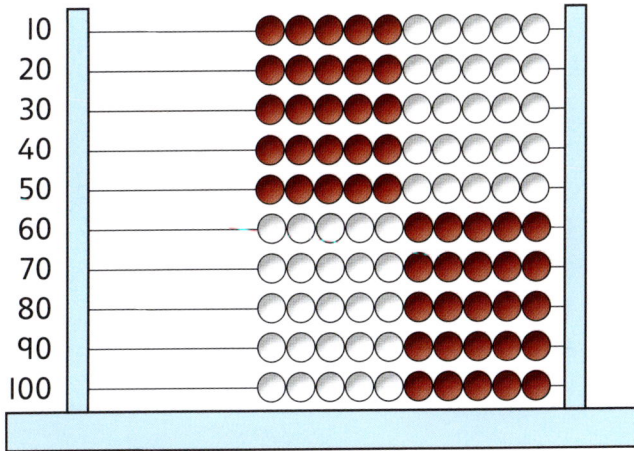

There are 100 beads in total.

I know that this is called a rekenrek.

b) There are 60 beads to the left.

There are 40 beads to the right.

There are 100 beads altogether.

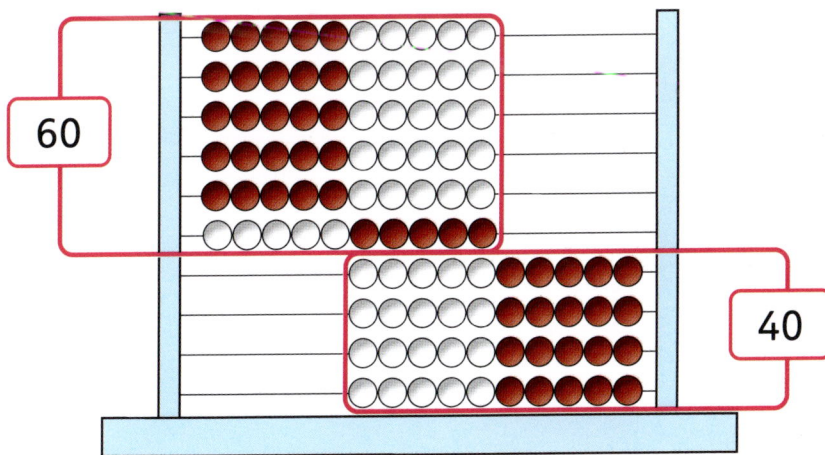

Two numbers that go together to make 100 are called **complements** to 100.

$60 + 40 = 100$

93

Think together

1 What number bonds to 100 are shown here?

a)

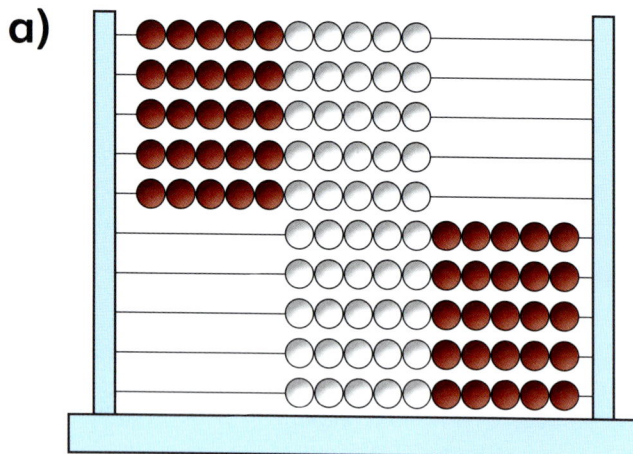

$\boxed{} + \boxed{} = 100$

b)

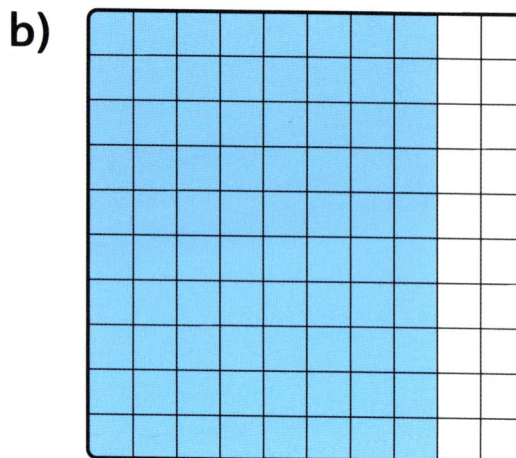

$\boxed{} + \boxed{} = 100$

2 Complete the number bond.

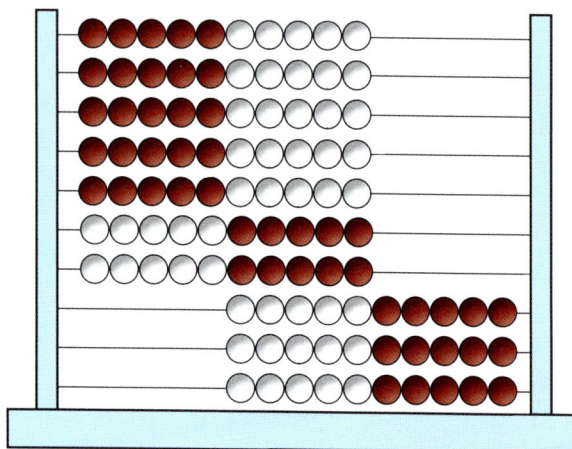

$70 + \boxed{} = 100$

CHALLENGE

3 Ola and Tariq are working out their 10 bonds to 100.

I have ten 10s rods and I will make two piles.

Ola

I am using a rekenrek and will put some beads to one end.

Tariq

Work out all the 10 bonds to 100.

Is there a way I can do this without missing any?

I will use my bonds to 10 to help me. There is a pattern.

95

→ Practice book 2A p68

Add and subtract 1s

Discover

1 **a)** How many corn on the cobs are on the table?

How many corn on the cobs are on the barbecue?

b) How many corn on the cobs are there altogether?

Share

I counted 10s then 1s.

a) There are 34 corn on the cobs on the table.

10 20 30 31 32 33 34

There are 5 corn on the cobs on the barbecue.

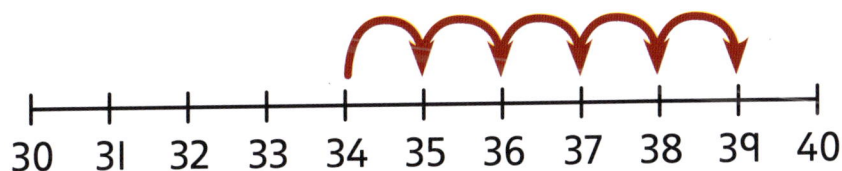

1 2 3 4 5

b)

$+$ $=$

30 31 32 33 34 35 36 37 38 39 40

There are 39 corn on the cobs in total.

I noticed that I could add the ones.
4 ones and 5 ones make 9 ones.

Think together

1   Use the base 10 to help you work out:

a) 41 + 6 = ☐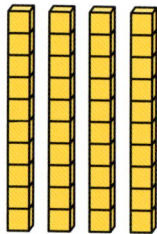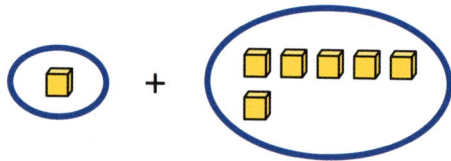

b) 52 + 4 = ☐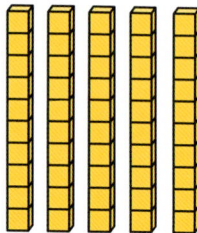

2   a) Work out the following.

| 42 + 5 | | 45 + 2 |

b) Work out the following.

47 − 2 = ☐   47 − 5 = ☐

I noticed something about the answers. I wonder why that is.

CHALLENGE

3 **a)** There are 26 eggs.

3 eggs are eaten.

How many eggs are left?

I wonder if I need to add the 1s.

I think you have to do something different here.

b) Work out the following.

18 – 3

28 – 3

38 – 3

48 – 3

I will try to find more like this.

What do you notice?

→ Practice book 2A p71

Add by making 10

Discover

Sam

Eva

1 a) How many stars has Sam found?

How many stars has Eva found?

Show each number on ten frames.

b) How many stars have they found altogether?

Share

a)

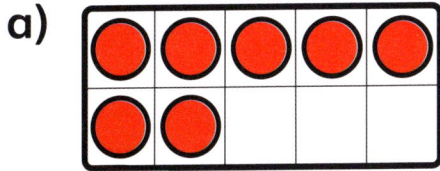

7

Sam has found 7 stars.

5

Eva has found 5 stars.

I used different coloured counters to show each number.

b) Add to find how many stars altogether.

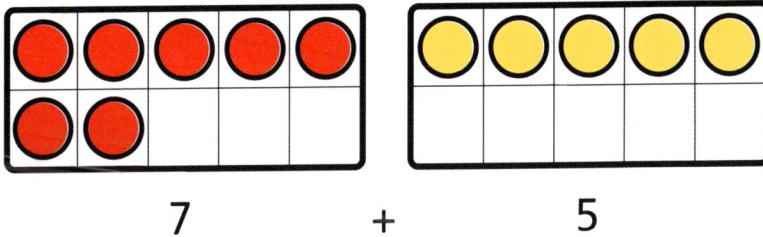

7   +   5

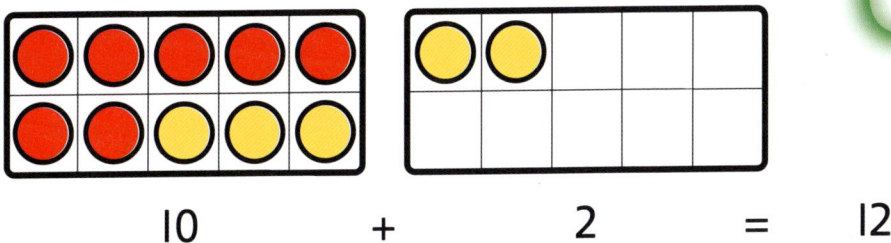

10   +   2   =   12

I added 3 to make 7 up to 10.

7 + 3 + 2 = 12

So 7 + 5 = 12

Think together

1 Work out 7 + 6.

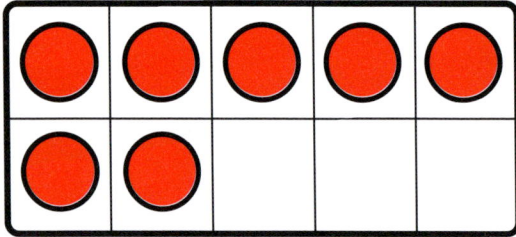 

7 + ☐ + ☐ = ☐

First, I will make 10.

2

Chen

I have 8 apples.

Kara

I have 6 apples.

How many apples do Chen and Kara have altogether?

CHALLENGE

3 Complete the number sentences.

Use the ten frames to help you.

a) $6 + 5 = \boxed{}$

b) $8 + 5 = \boxed{}$

c) $9 + 5 = \boxed{}$

d) $5 + 7 = \boxed{}$

We need to break up 5 for each number sentence.

Then we can find the number that makes 10.

103

→ Practice book 2A p74

Add using a number line

Discover

There are 9 jumpers in this box.

Lost property

1 a) How many jumpers are in the box?

How many are on the ground?

Make each number.

b) How many are there altogether?

Share

a) There are 9 in the box.   There are 4 on the ground.

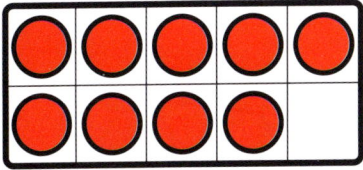   

b) Add by making 10 to find how many altogether.

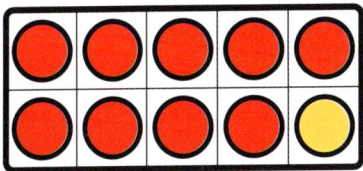   +

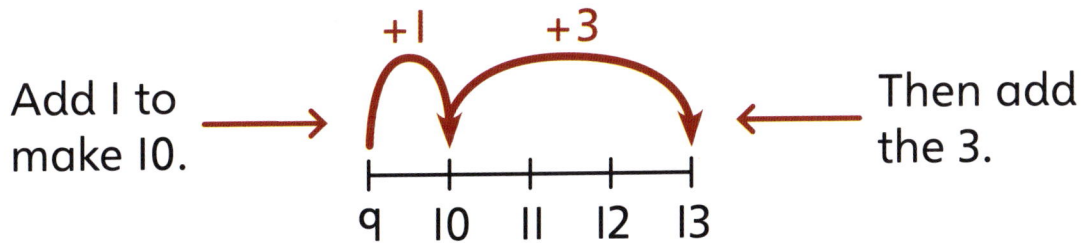

Add 1 to make 10.   Then add the 3.

$9 + 1 + 3 = 13$

So $9 + 4 = 13$

There are 13 jumpers altogether.

I used a number line to help me.

105

Think together

1 Work out 8 + 5.

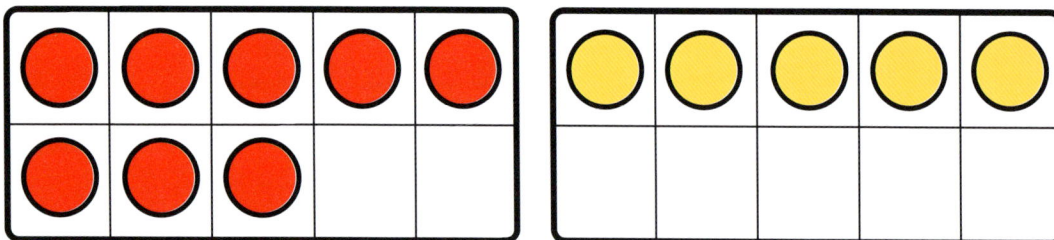

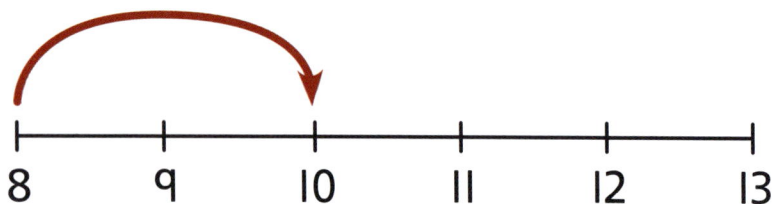

8   9   10   11   12   13

I will make the numbers on ten frames and then use a number line to help me.

2 Work out these sums.

| 7 + 6 | 9 + 5 |

| 8 + 3 | 6 + 8 |

CHALLENGE

3 Seth and Molly are working out 5 + 7.

I used a number line and started at 5.

Seth

I started at 7 and then added on 5.

Molly

I wonder whether it is better to start on 5 or 7.

Do they have the same answer?

→ Practice book 2A p77

Add three I-digit numbers

Discover

I **a)** How many fingers and thumbs is each child holding up?

b) How many fingers and thumbs are being held up altogether?

Share

a)

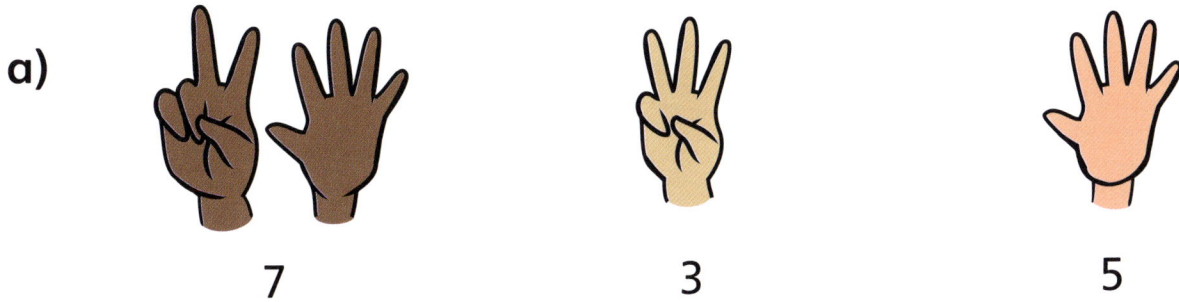

7   3   5

b)

I made each number using a ten frame.

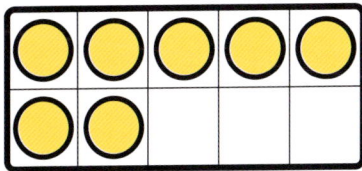   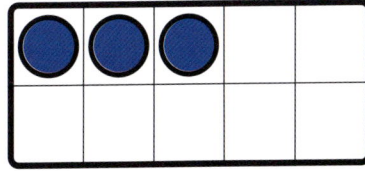   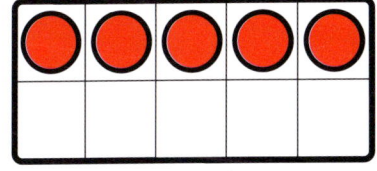

7   3   5

I saw that 7 + 3 = 10.
Then I did 10 + 5 = 15.

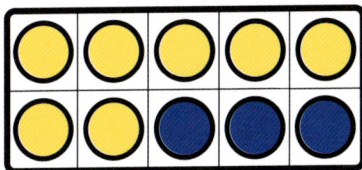   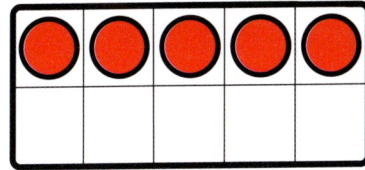

15 fingers and thumbs are being held up altogether.

Think together

1 How many fingers are there?

a)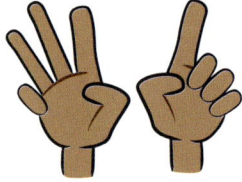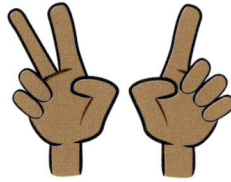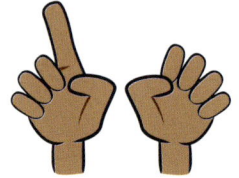

b)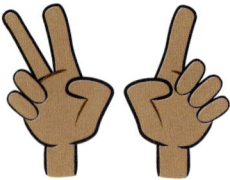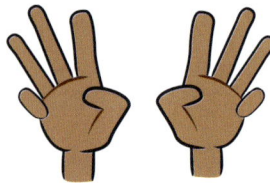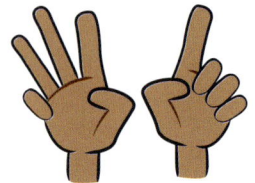

I will make each number on a ten frame to help me add.

2 What is the missing number?

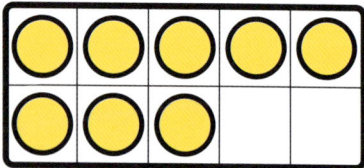 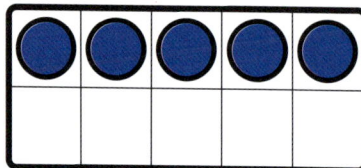 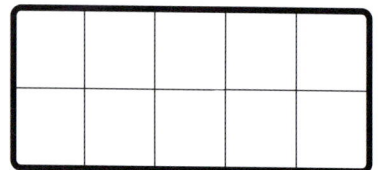

8 + 5 + ▢ = 19

CHALLENGE

3 Work out 5 + 7 + 5.

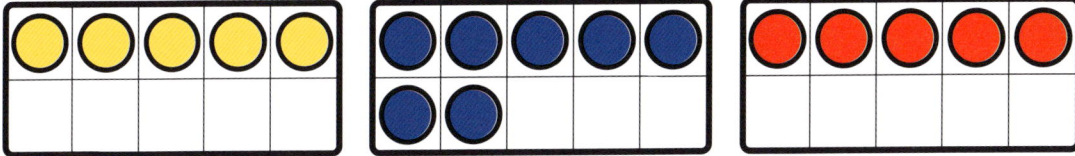

I can do this by first adding 5 + 7 and then adding 5 more.

I think that using number bonds to 10 helps.

Which method do you prefer?

111

→ Practice book 2A p80

Add to the next 10

Discover

1 **a)** How many cups are there in total?

b) How many more cups are needed to finish the middle tower?

Now solve $23 +$ ☐ $= 30$.

Share

a)

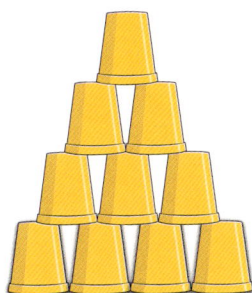
10

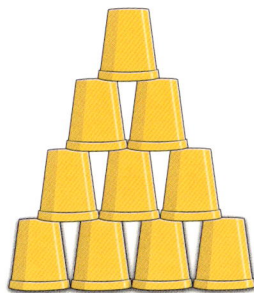
20

21   22   23

b)

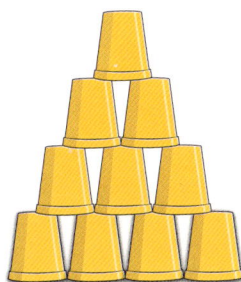

I used a number bond to 10 to help me.

3 + 7 = 10

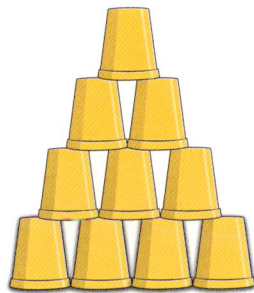

+7

23 + 7 = 30

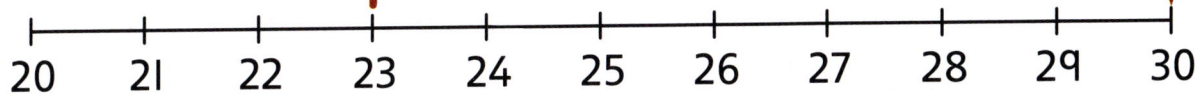
20   21   22   23   24   25   26   27   28   29   30

Think together

1 Meg has made 28.

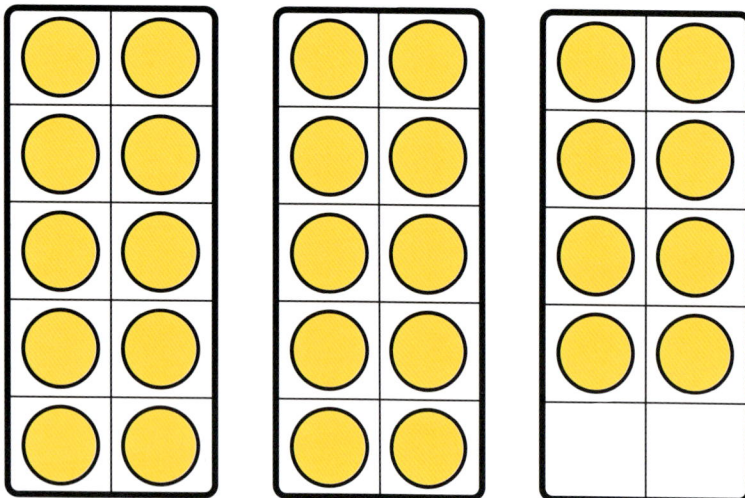

Work out

$8 + \boxed{} = 10$

$28 + \boxed{} = 30$

2 Use the ten frame to complete the following.

$3 + \boxed{} = 10$

$33 + \boxed{} = 40$

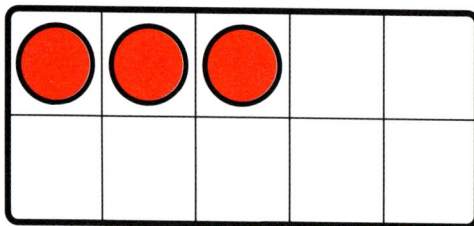

$43 + \boxed{} = 50$

$73 + \boxed{} = 80$

3 Add to the next 10.

a)

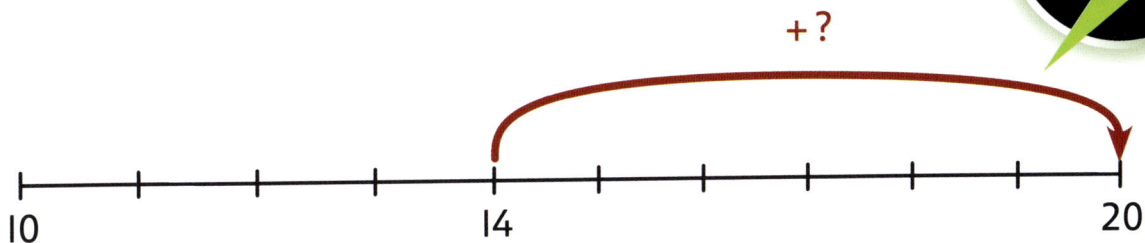

$14 +$ ☐ $= 20$

b)

60	
55	?

$55 +$ ☐ $= 60$

c)

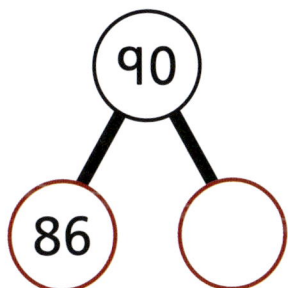

$86 +$ ☐ $= 90$

I will use a ten frame.

I will use my number bonds to 10.

115

→ Practice book 2A p83

Add across a 10

Discover

1 **a)** There are 10 chairs in each full stack.

How many chairs are stacked?

Show this number on ten frames.

b) How many chairs are there in total?

Share

a) There are 4 full stacks of chairs.

There are 5 more chairs stacked.

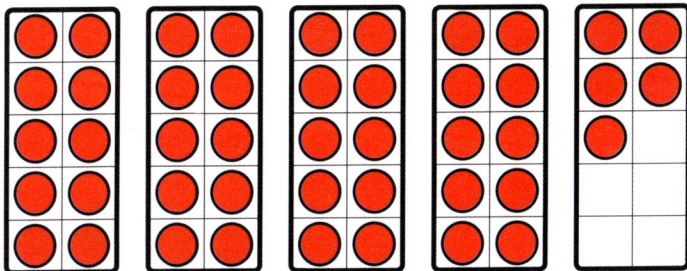

There are 45 chairs stacked.

b) There are 7 more chairs that need stacking.

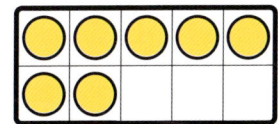

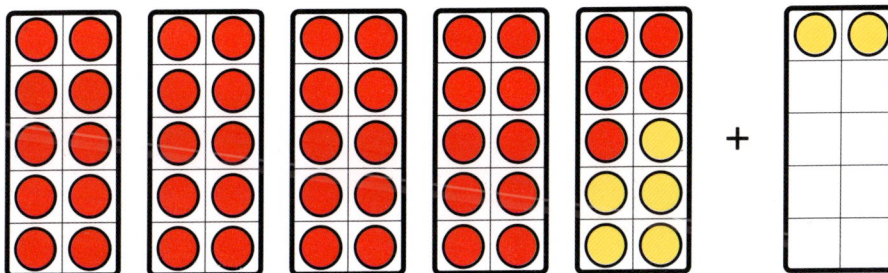

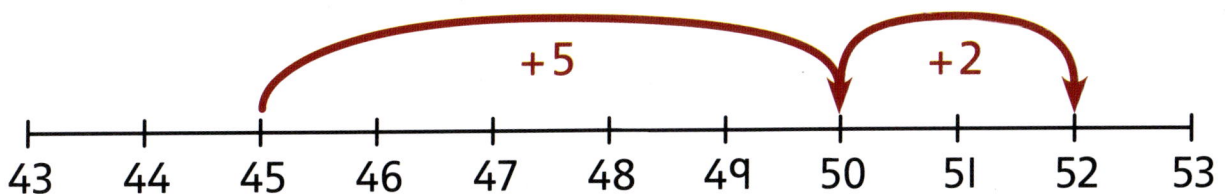

+

$45 + 7 = 45 + 5 + 2 = 52$ chairs in total.

Think together

1 How many stars are there in total?

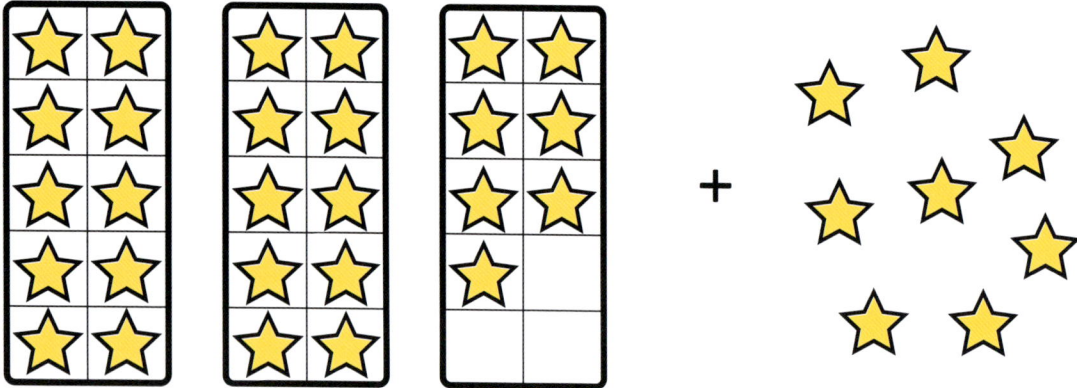

27 + 8 = 27 + ☐ + ☐ = ☐

2 Work out 34 + 8.

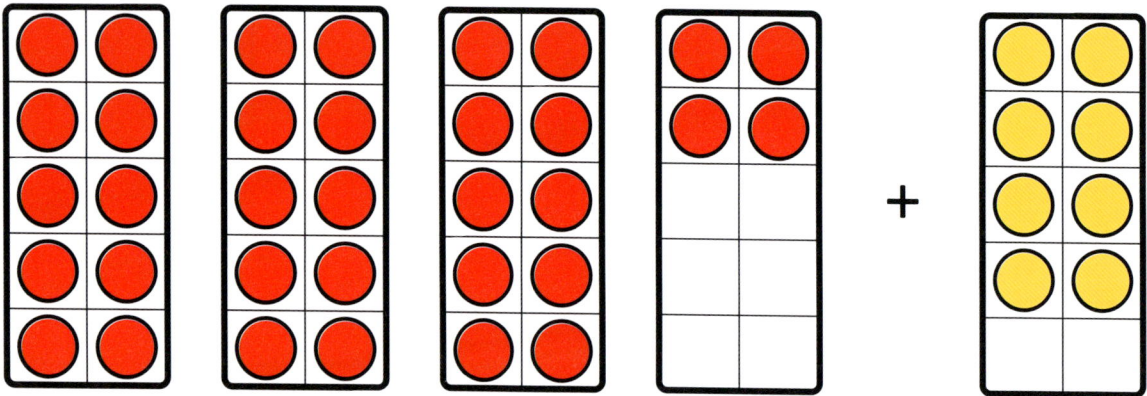

34 + 8 = 34 + ☐ + ☐ = ☐

CHALLENGE

3 Here are some calculation cards.

| 42 + 6 | 47 + 6 |

| 43 + 6 | 49 + 6 |

Which of these answers will be greater than 50?

I will work out the answer to each question to check.

I can tell without doing any working out.

→ Practice book 2A p86

Subtract across a 10

Discover

1 **a)** How many pencils are there?

Show this number on ten frames.

b) 5 children take a pencil.

How many pencils are left?

Share

a)

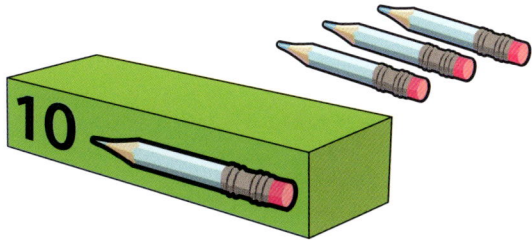

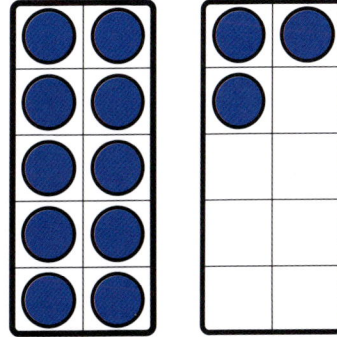

There are 13 pencils.

b) 5 children take a pencil.

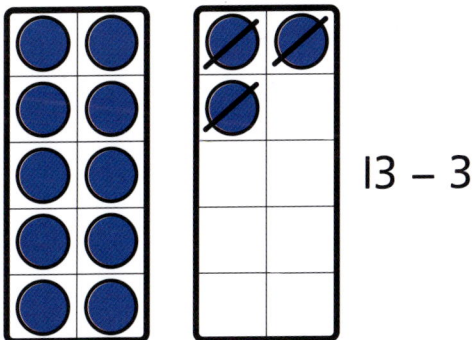

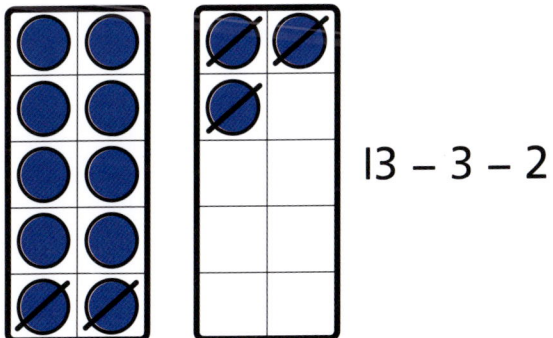

$13 - 3$

$13 - 3 - 2$

$13 - 5 = 8$

There are 8 pencils left.

I subtracted 5 from 13 to work out how many were left.

I subtracted 3 first, then I subtracted 2.

Think together

1 The teacher has 12 rubbers.

5 children need rubbers.

How many are left?

12 – ☐ – ☐ = ☐

12 – 5 = ☐

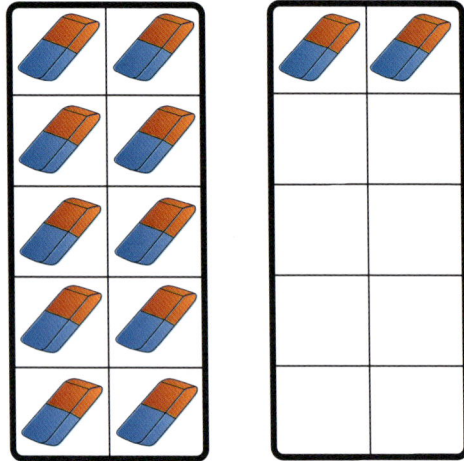

2 Work out 14 – 8 = ☐.

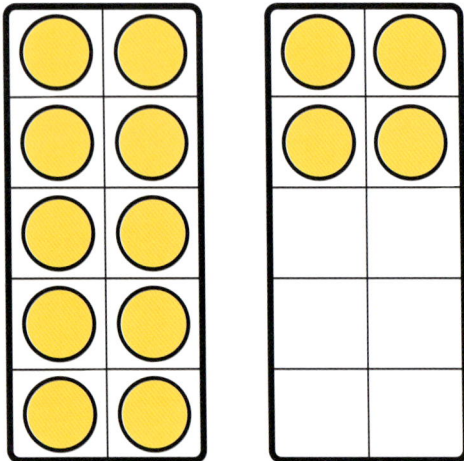

14 – ☐ – ☐ = ☐

CHALLENGE

3 Leo is showing 13 – 7 on a ten frame.

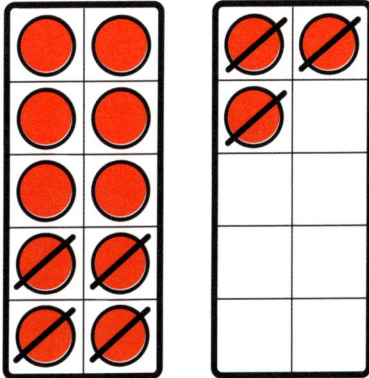

Dan wants to use a number line to work out 13 – 7.

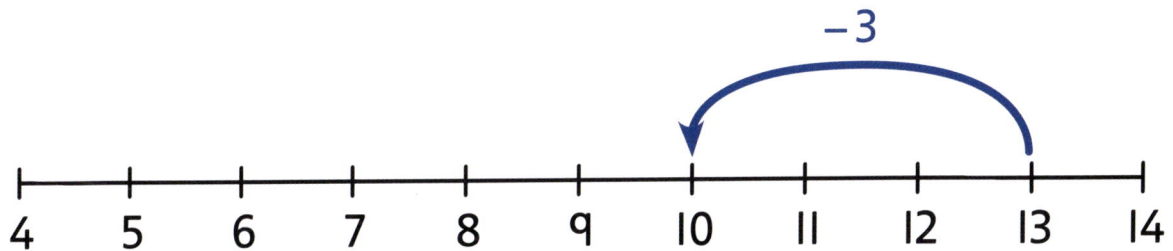

$$-3$$

```
4   5   6   7   8   9   10   11   12   13   14
```

What other jump does Dan have to make?

I can use what Leo did to help me.

I like the number line. I'm going to use it to check my answers to the other questions.

123

→ Practice book 2A p89

Subtract from a 10

Discover

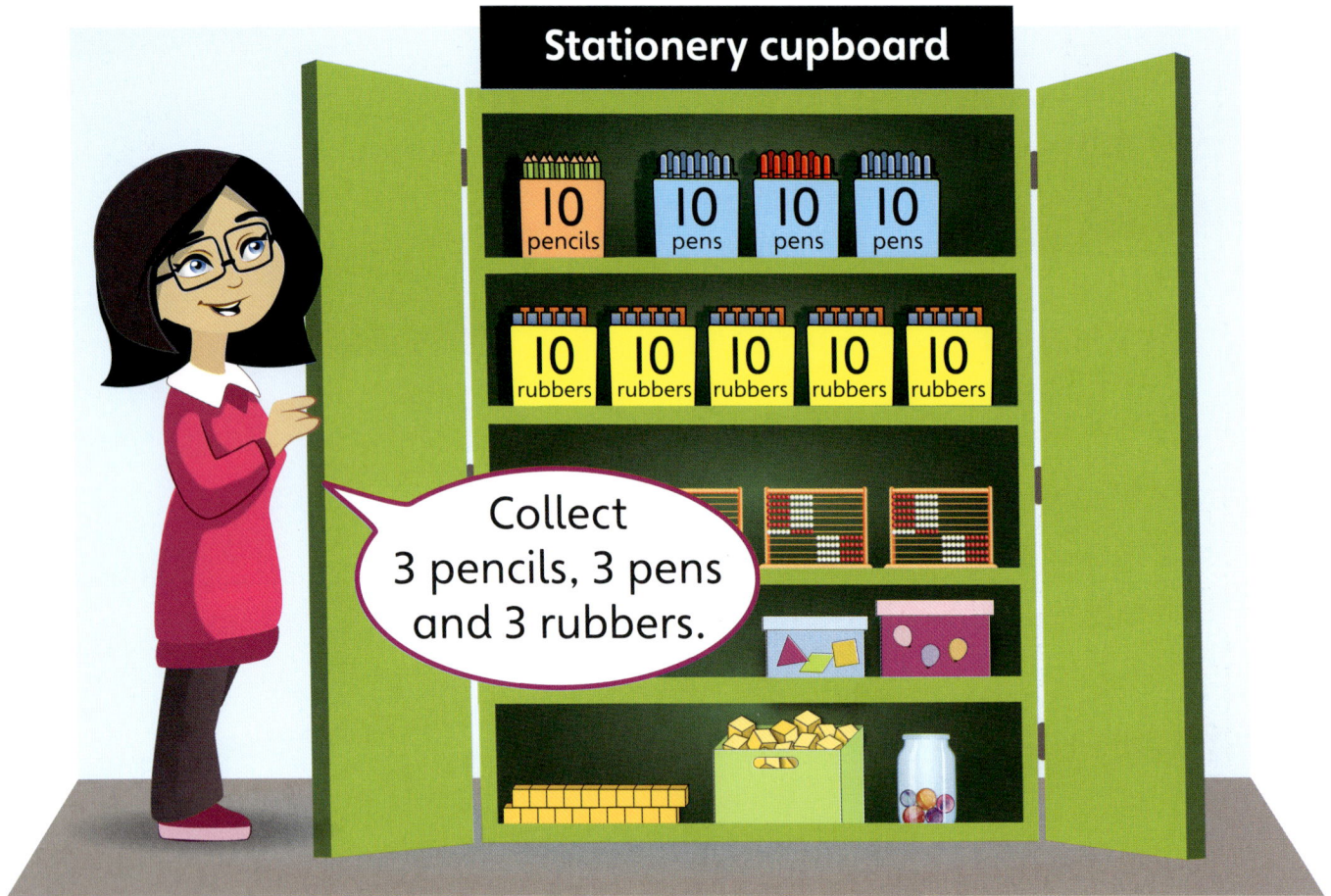

1 **a)** How many pencils will be left in the pack?

b) How many pens will be left?

How many rubbers will be left?

Share

a)

$10 - 3 = 7$

I used my number bonds to 10.

There will be 7 pencils left in the pack.

b)

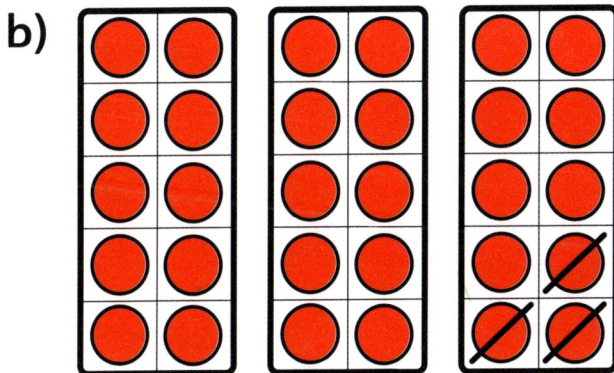

$30 - 3 = 27$

There will be 27 pens left.

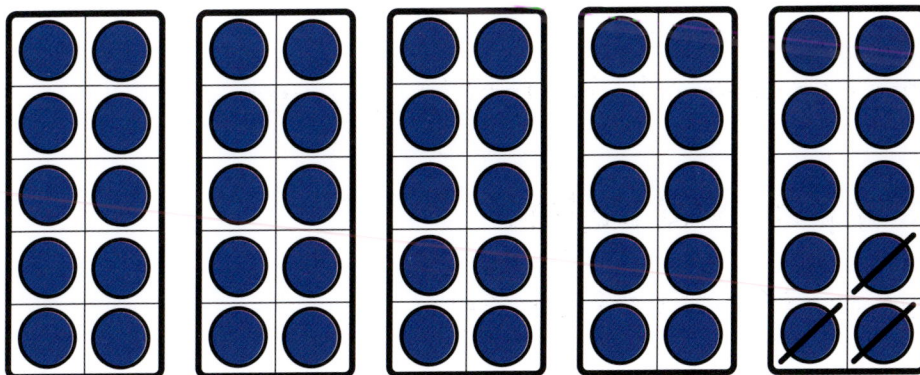

$50 - 3 = 47$

There will be 47 rubbers left.

125

Think together

1. Subtract 8 counters.

   How many are left?

   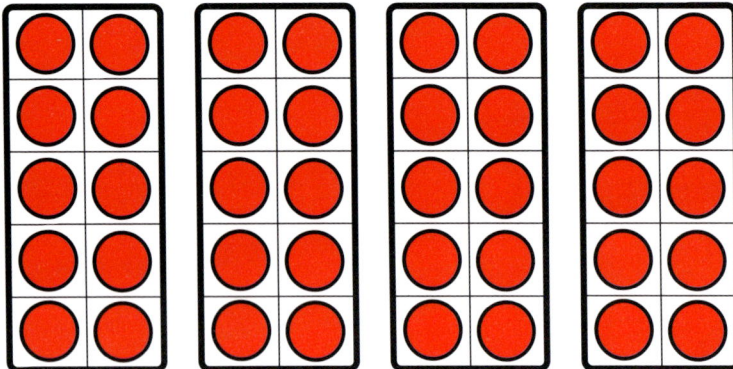

   $40 - 8 = \boxed{}$

2. There are 30 apples on a tree.

   a) On Monday, 5 apples fall off.

      How many are left on the tree?

      $30 - \boxed{} = \boxed{}$

   b) On Wednesday, there are 23 apples on the tree.

      How many have fallen off in total?

      $30 - \boxed{} = \boxed{}$

CHALLENGE

3 Calculate the missing numbers.

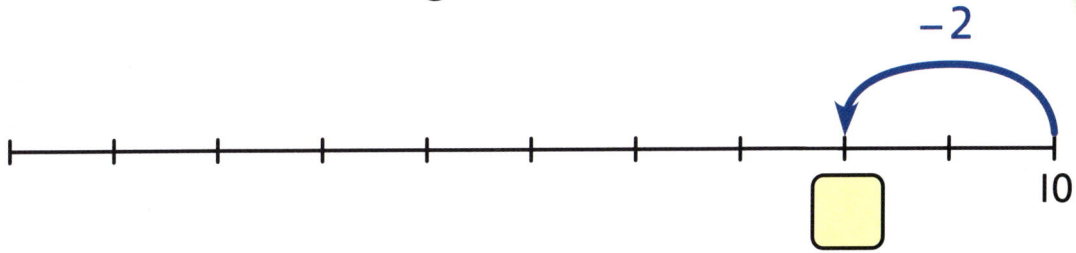

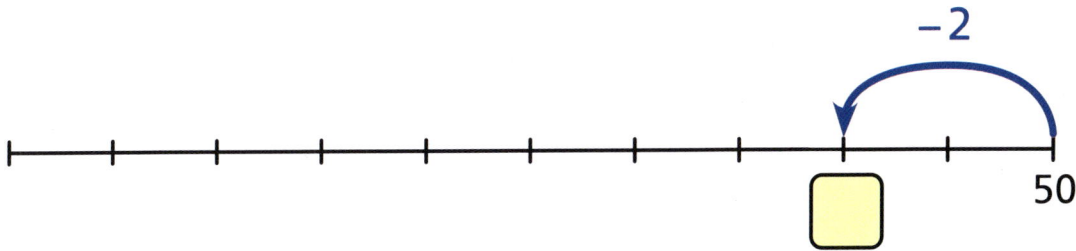

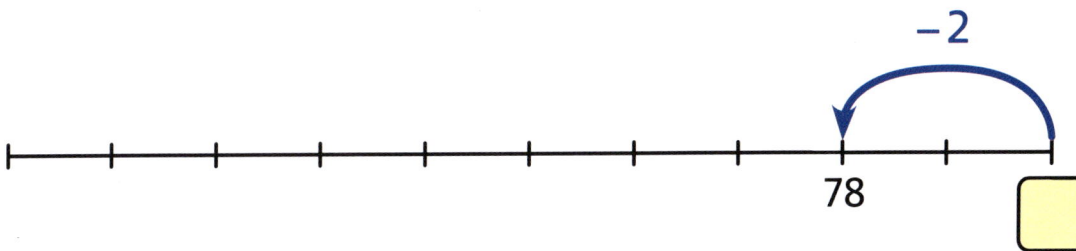

−2

[ ]   10

−2

[ ]   50

−2

78   [ ]

I will use my number bonds to 10.

But, how do number bonds help with subtraction?

→ Practice book 2A p92

Subtract a 1-digit number from a 2-digit number – across 10

Discover

Class B: 35 children

Away today:

Amira
Hanan
Emma
James
Ali
Bob

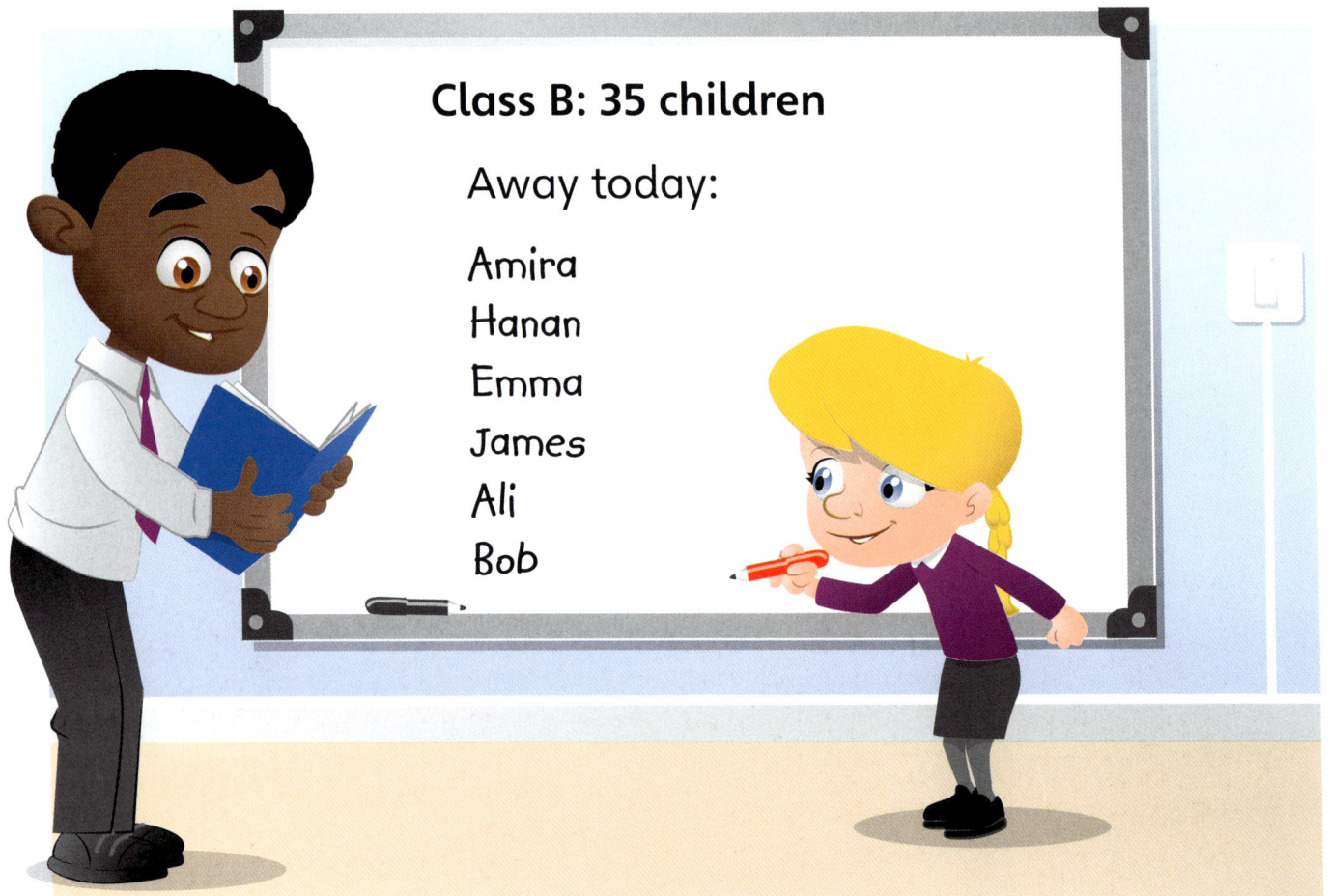

1 **a)** Show 35 on ten frames.

   b) Today 6 children are away.

   How many children are in Class B today?

Share

a) There are 35 children in Class B.

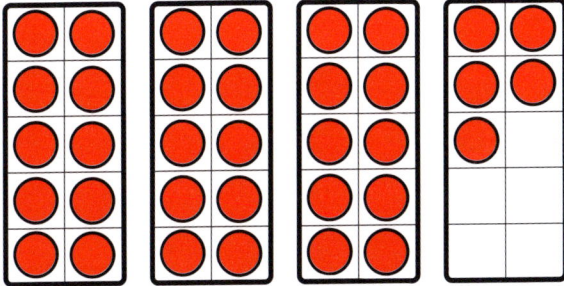

b)

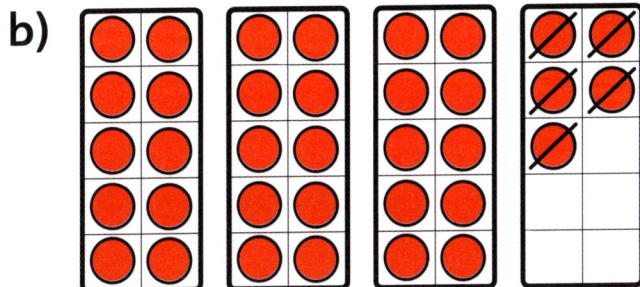

35 − 5 = 30

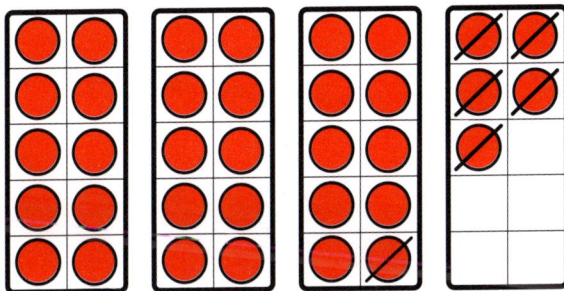

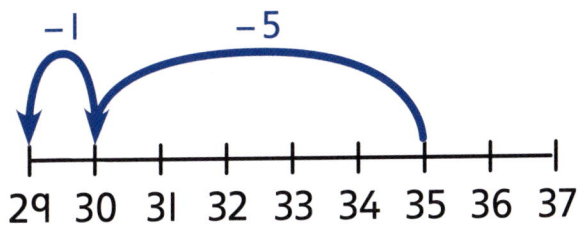

35 − 5 − 1 = 29

There are 29 children in Class B today.

> We can do the subtraction in two parts. We subtract 5 first.

> I jumped back to 30 first then jumped 1 more back.

129

Think together

1   Work out 24 − 6.

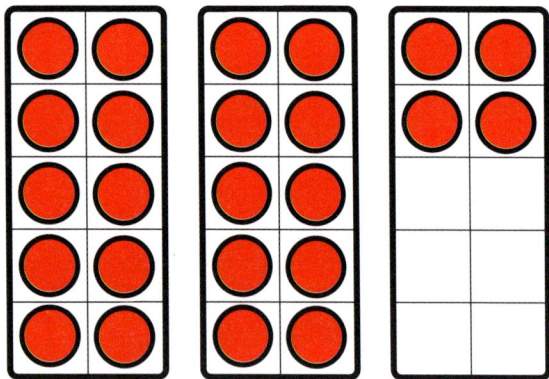

24 − ☐ − ☐ = ☐

So 24 − 6 = ☐

2   Complete these number sentences.

a)   34 − 7 = 34 − ☐ − ☐ = ☐

b)   46 − 7 = 46 − ☐ − ☐ = ☐

c)   55 − 7 = 55 − ☐ − ☐ = ☐

I find it easier to draw a ten frame.

I will make the numbers on a ten frame to help me.

3 What is the same in these calculations?

What is different?

CHALLENGE

| 37 – 4 | | 34 – 7 |

26 27 28 29 30 31 32 33 34 35 36 37 38

Use a number line to help you.

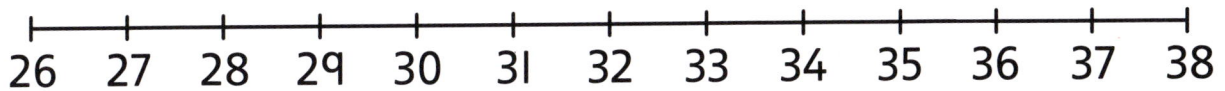

These calculations have the same digits in. I think they answer the same question.

I am not sure. I think they give different answers. I wonder why the answers are different.

131

→ Practice book 2A p95

End of unit check

Your teacher will ask you these questions.

1 Which two numbers do not add up to make 100?

A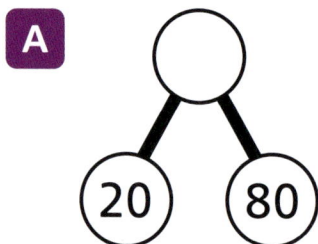
20 80

C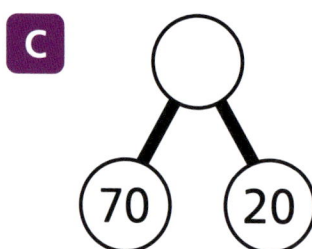
70 20

B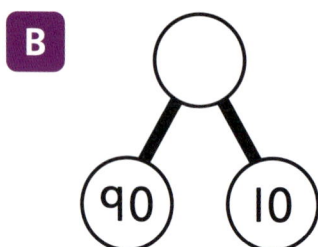
90 10

D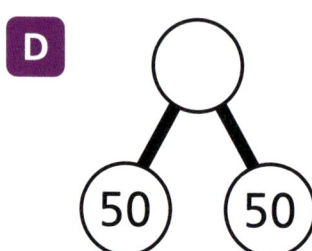
50 50

2 What is 8 + 5?

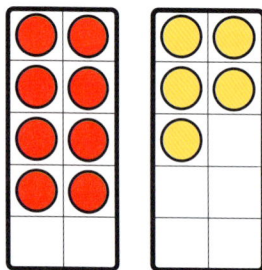

A 3   **B** 10   **C** 13   **D** 15

3 What is 20 + 60?

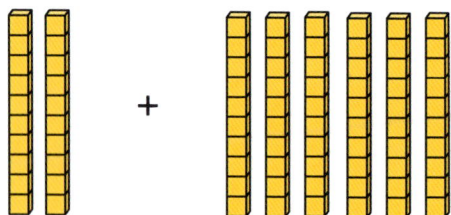
+

A 8   **B** 80   **C** 90   **D** 100

4 Work out 12 – 8.

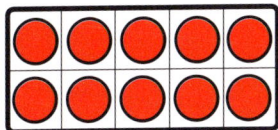 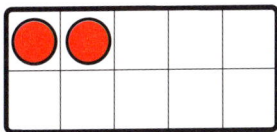

A 20   **B** 10   **C** 6   **D** 4

5 A box contains 64 pencils.

There are 8 yellow pencils. The rest are green.

Which calculation shows how many green pencils there are?

A 64 – 8   **C** 64 – 9

B 64 + 8   **D** 8 – 64

6 What is the difference between 35 and 9?

A 26   **B** 27   **C** 34   **D** 45

Think!

What methods would you use to work out the following?

36 + 2   36 – 2

36 + 9   36 – 9

These words will help you.

tens   ones   add

total   subtract

133

→ Practice book 2A p98

Unit 3
Addition and subtraction ②

In this unit we will …

⚡ Add two 2-digit numbers
⚡ Subtract 2-digit numbers
⚡ Find the difference between two numbers
⚡ Solve missing number problems

How many more rubbers are there than pencils?

Use the number line to find out.

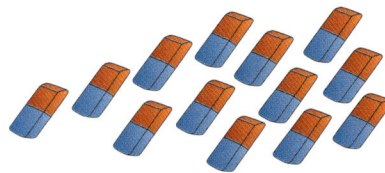

We will need some maths words. Do you remember any of them?

total   tens   ones

subtract   difference

10 more   10 less

bar model   represent

Base 10 equipment is useful. Use it to find the total of 16 + 7.

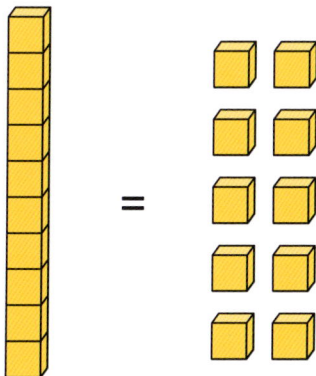

=

10 more, 10 less

Discover

1 a) Jen has 43 points. She then gets **10 more** points.

How many does she have now?

b) Tom has 57 points. He then loses 10 points.

How many points does Tom have now?

Share

a) Jen has 43 points.

10 more than 43 is 53.

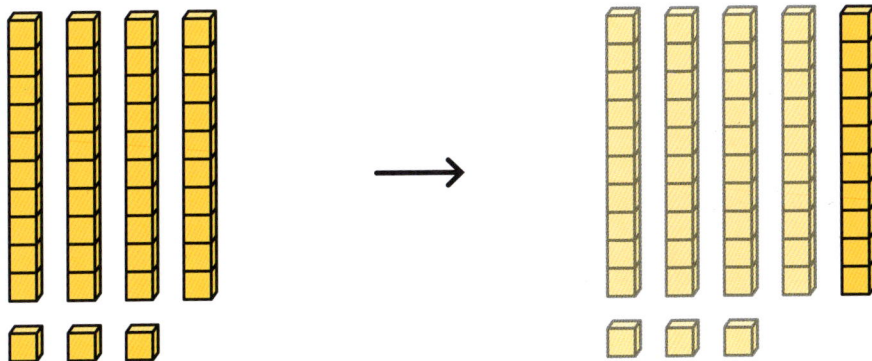

Jen has 53 points now.

b) Tom has 57 points.

10 less than 57 is 47.

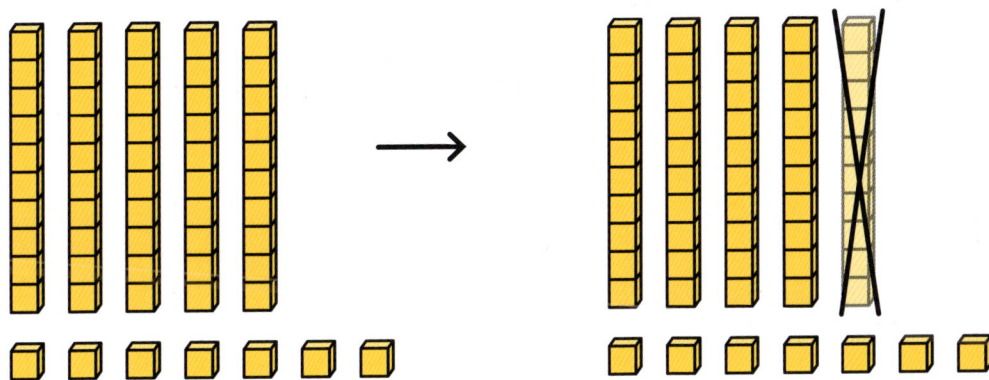

Tom has 47 points now.

> I can see that the number of 10s went up or down by 1.

Think together

1 How many points does Jen have now?

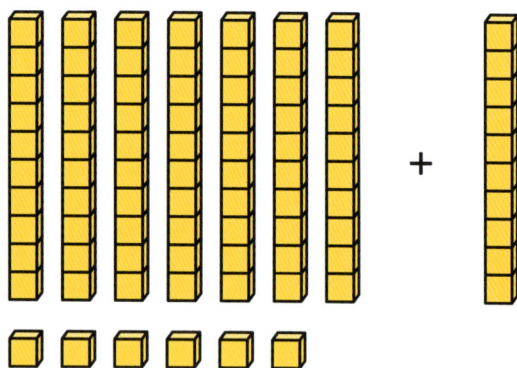

+

10 more than 76 is [ ].

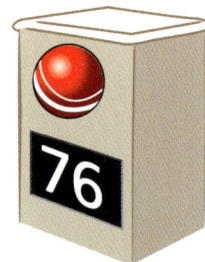

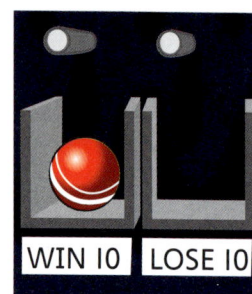

WIN 10   LOSE 10

2 **a)** Copy and complete the number track.

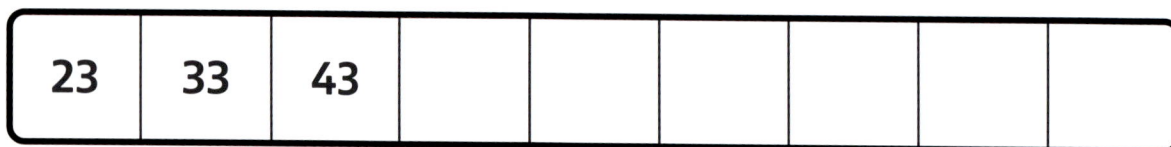

23	33	43						

b) Copy and complete the number track.

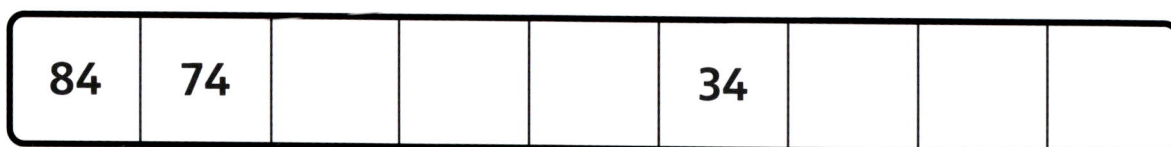

84	74				34			

3 Here is a 100 square.

CHALLENGE

1	2	3	4	5	6	7	8	9	10
11	12	13	14	15	16	17	18	19	20
21	22	23	24	25	26	27	28	29	30
31	32	33	34	35	36	37	38	39	40
41	42	43	44	45	46	47	48	49	50
51	52	53	54	55	56	57	58	59	60
61	62	63	64	65	66	67	68	69	70
71	72	73	74	75	76	77	78	79	80
81	82	83	84	85	86	87	88	89	90
91	92	93	94	95	96	97	98	99	100

I will count on 10 from 73.

a) Point to 73.

Point to 10 more than 73.

What do you notice?

b) Point to 64.

Point to 10 less than 64.

What do you notice?

I think there is a quicker way.

c) Work out:

10 more than 58 is ☐.

35 is 10 more than ☐.

10 less than 99 is ☐.

→ Practice book 2A p100

Add and subtract 10s

Discover

1 **a)** How many toffee apples are on the table?

How many toffee apples are on the ground?

b) How many toffee apples are there in total?

Share

a) There are 16 toffee apples on the table.

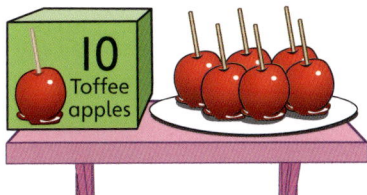

There are 30 toffee apples on the ground.

b) There are 6 ones in total.

There are 4 tens in total.

T	O	T	O

I used base 10 equipment to make each number.

I know that 1 ten and 3 tens makes 4 tens.

$16 + 30 = 46$

There are 46 toffee apples in total.

Think together

1 Work out

a) 25 + 30 = ☐

b) 36 + 40 = ☐

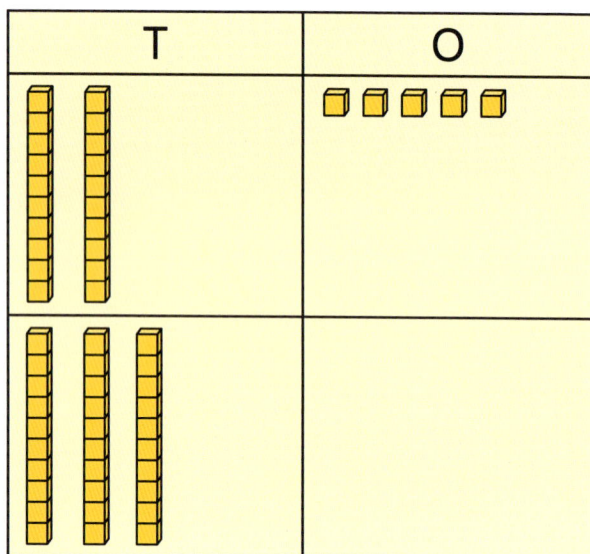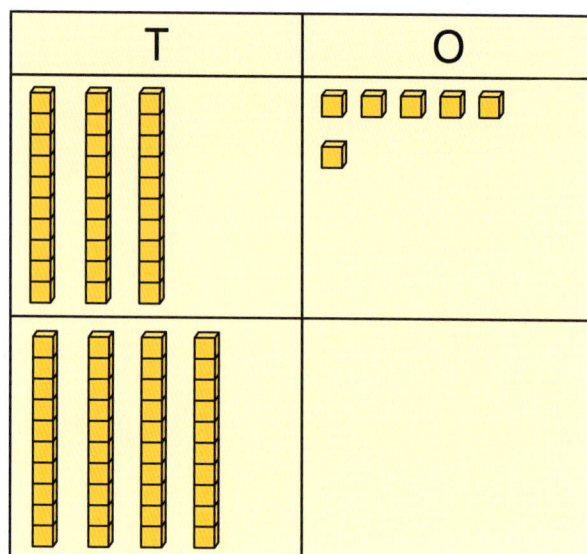

2 a) Work out 51 – 20 = ☐.

b) Work out 76 – 50 = ☐.

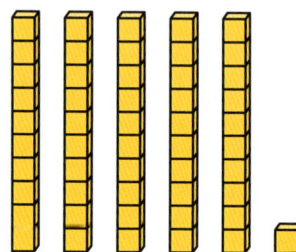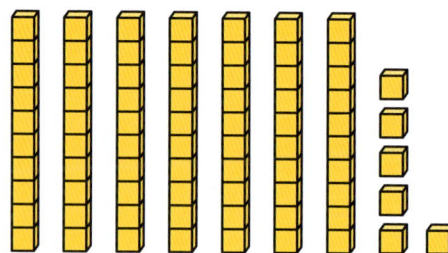

3 **a)** Two children are working out 36 + 20.

CHALLENGE

Ben

36   46   56

Asha

3 tens + 2 tens = 5 tens.
The answer is 56.

Explain each method.

Do they both work?

I'm going to try
to work these out
in my head.

b) Use Ben's or Asha's method to work out

35 + 20

17 + 60

35 + 30

24 + 60

35 + 40

31 + 60

143

→ Practice book 2A p103

Add two 2-digit numbers – add 10s and add 1s

Discover

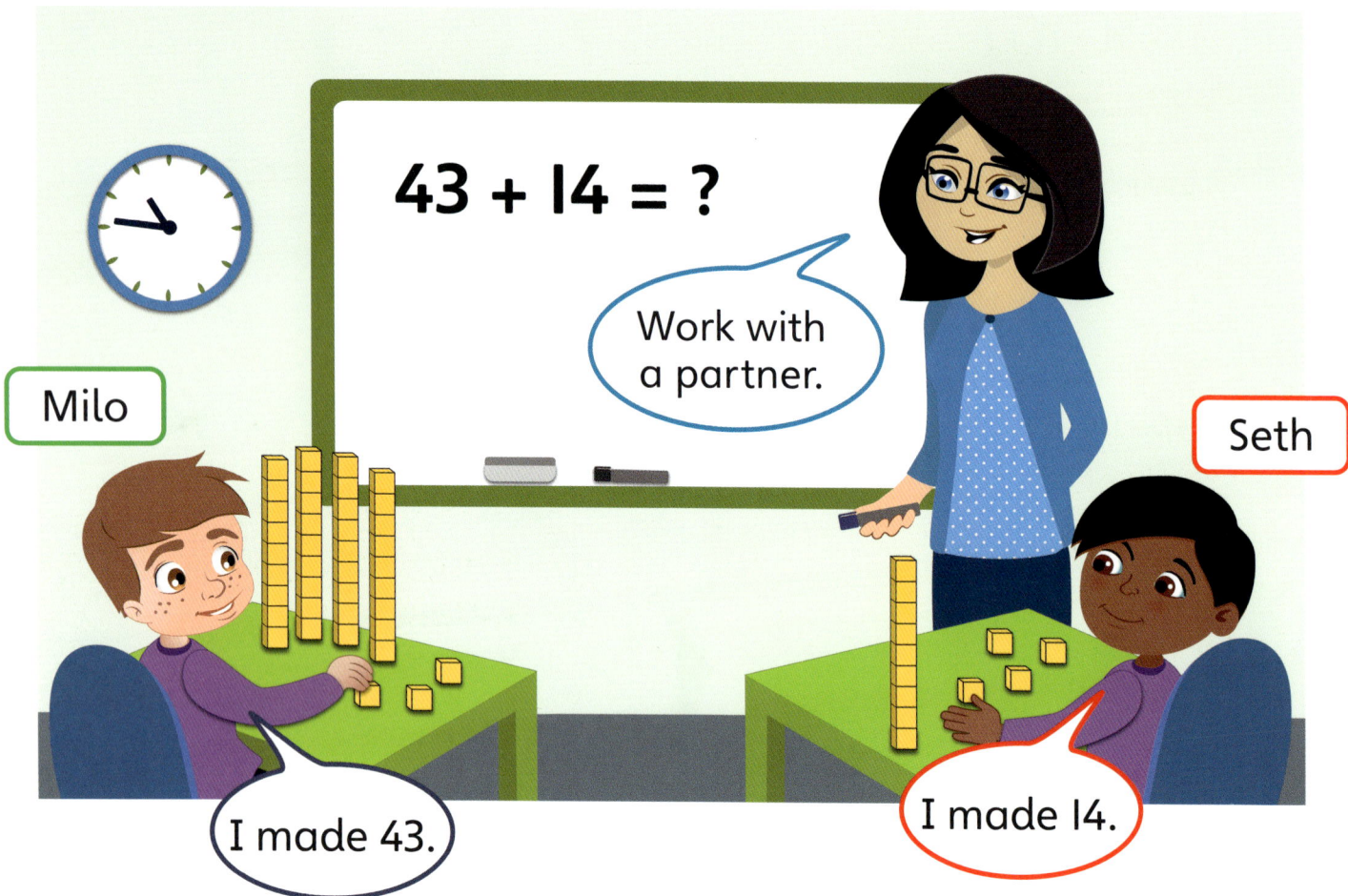

I **a)** How can Milo and Seth find the answer?

b) Work out the addition

43 + 14 = ☐

Share

a) Milo has 4 tens.

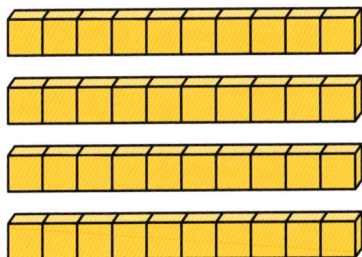

Seth has 1 ten.

4 tens + 1 ten = 5 tens

Milo has 3 ones.

Seth has 4 ones.

3 ones + 4 ones = 7 ones

The answer is 57.

b) 43 + 14 = 57

T	O

I added the 10s:
40 + 10 = 50.
Then I added the 1s:
3 + 4 = 7.

145

Think together

1 **a)** Make or draw 42. Make or draw 25.

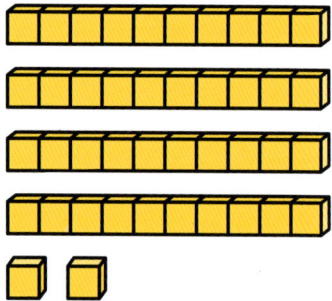

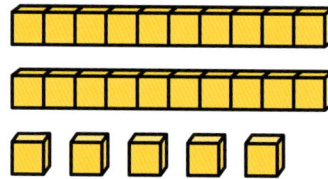

b) Work out $42 + 25 = \boxed{}$.

I will add the 1s.

I will add the 10s.

2 Complete the number sentences.

$31 + 26 = \boxed{}$ $18 + 61 = \boxed{}$ $44 + 55 = \boxed{}$

I will use my number bonds.

3 **a)** Help Maya, Kara and Jack solve

35 + 27 = ☐.

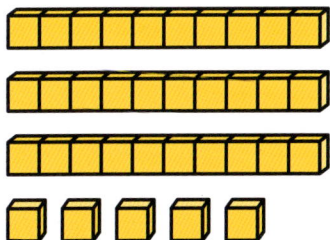 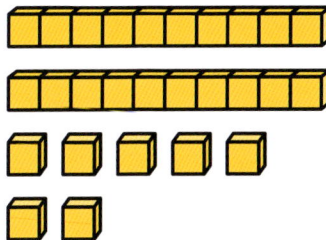

Maya

Jack

5 ones and
7 ones make
12 ones.

3 tens and
2 tens make
5 tens.

Is it fifty-twelve?

Kara

b) Work out these additions:

24 + 18 = ☐

51 + 29 = ☐

47 + 46 = ☐

147

→ Practice book 2A p106

Add two 2-digit numbers – add more 10s then more 1s

Discover

I have 23 parcels in here.

Charlie

Mia

1 **a)** Charlie puts his parcels into the van.

How many parcels are now in the van?

b) Next, Mia puts her parcels into the van.

How many parcels are now in the van?

Share

a) There are 23 parcels in the van.

Then Charlie adds 10 parcels.

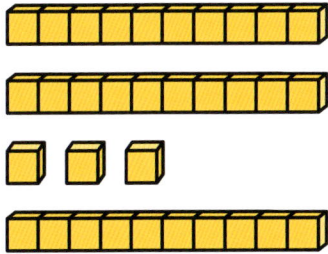

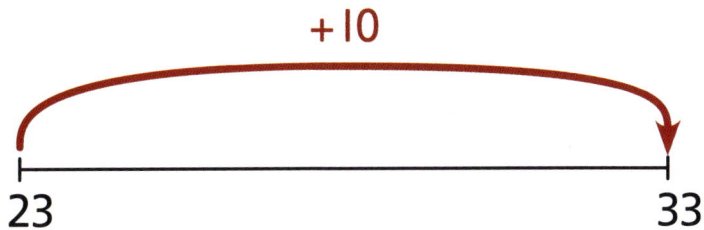

$$23 + 10 = 33$$

There are now 33 parcels in the van.

b) Now Mia adds 2 more parcels.

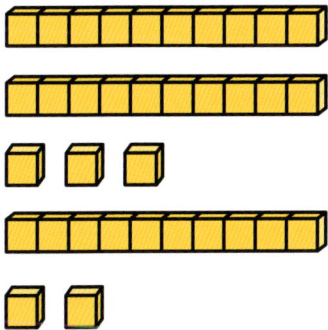

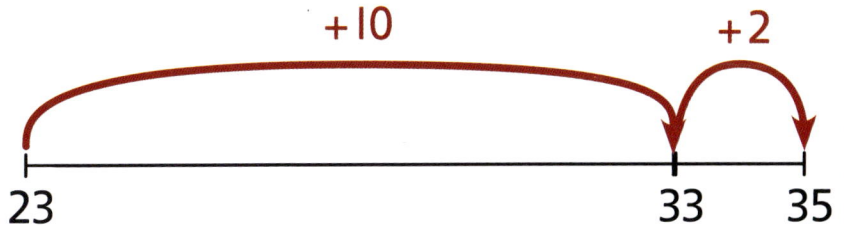

$$33 + 2 = 35$$

There are now 35 parcels in the van.

I drew a number line to help me.

I used base 10 equipment to help me.

Think together

1 **a)** Make or draw 35.

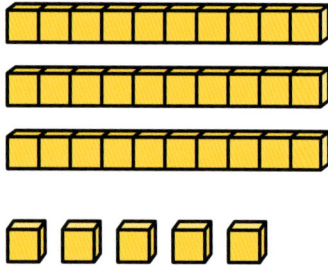

b) Add 13 to 35.

First add 10.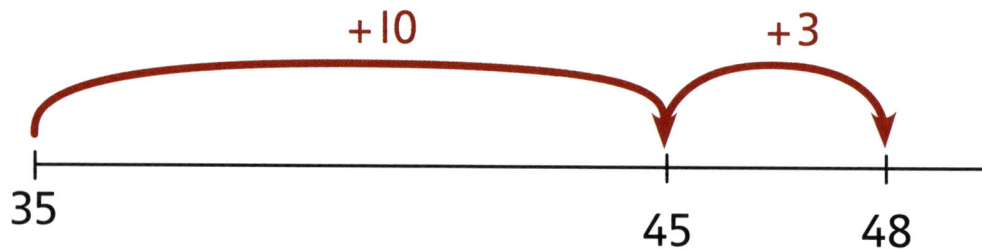

Then add 3.

Complete 35 + 13 = ☐.

2 Work out 32 + 24.

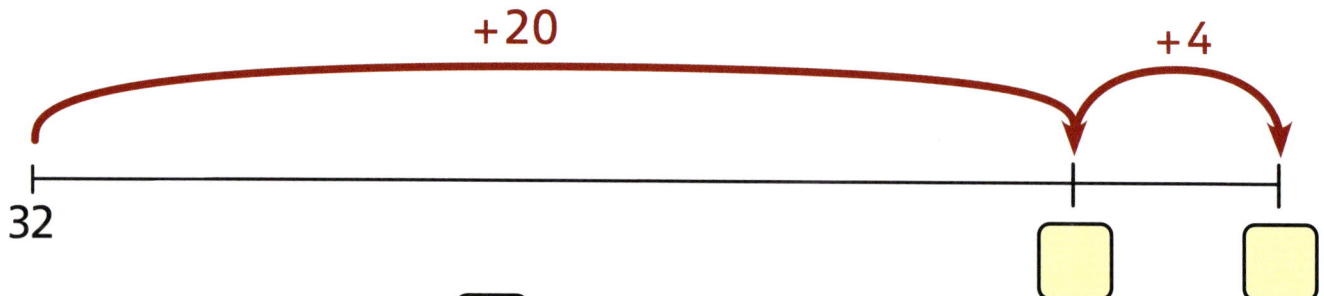

Complete 32 + 24 = ☐.

3 **a)** Help Maya, Kara and Jack solve $38 + 25$.

Add 20.

Now add 5.

Start at 38.

Maya

Kara

Jack

+20   +2 +3

38   58 60   63

$38 + 25 = \boxed{}$

I always draw a number line.

b) Work out these additions:

$34 + 10 + 8 = \boxed{}$

$56 + 29 = \boxed{}$

$47 + 37 = \boxed{}$

I can solve some in my head.

151

→ Practice book 2A p109

Subtract a 2-digit number from a 2-digit number – not across 10

Discover

1 **a)** Anna takes the eggs that she needs.

How many eggs are left?

b) Then Seth takes the eggs that he needs.

How many eggs are left?

Share

a) Anna and Seth have 25 eggs in total.

Anna uses 10 eggs.

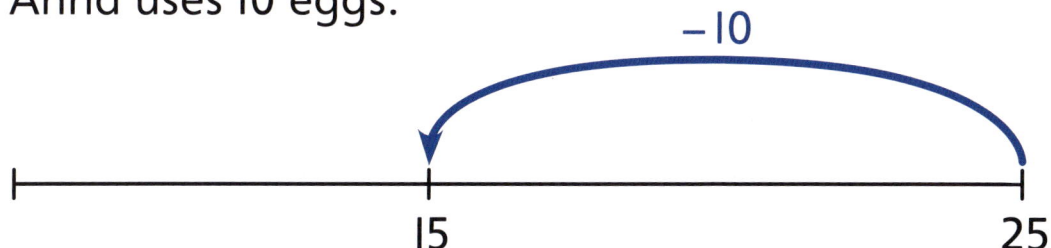

$25 - 10 = 15$

There are now 15 eggs left.

b) Seth needs 2 eggs.

$15 - 2 = 13$

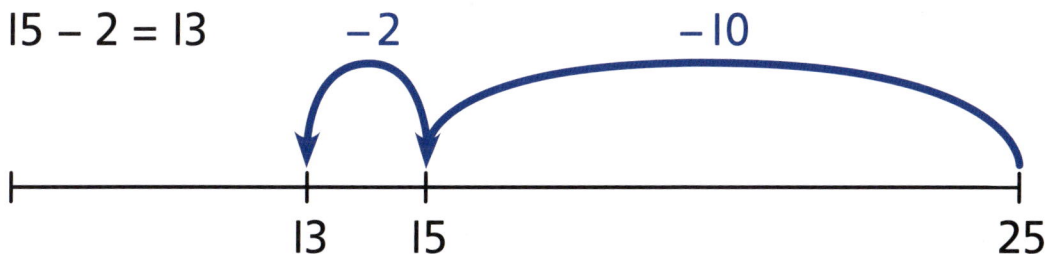

There are 13 eggs left.

We can use base 10 equipment.

$25 - 10 - 2 = 13$

There are 13 eggs left.

Think together

1 a) Work out 38 – 10.

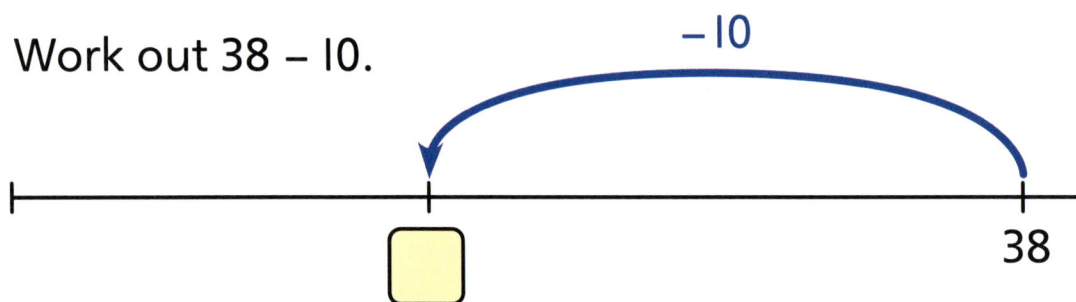

-10

⌐⌐⌐⌐⌐⌐⌐⌐⌐⌐⌐⌐⌐⌐⌐ 38

[ ]

b) Work out 38 – 15.

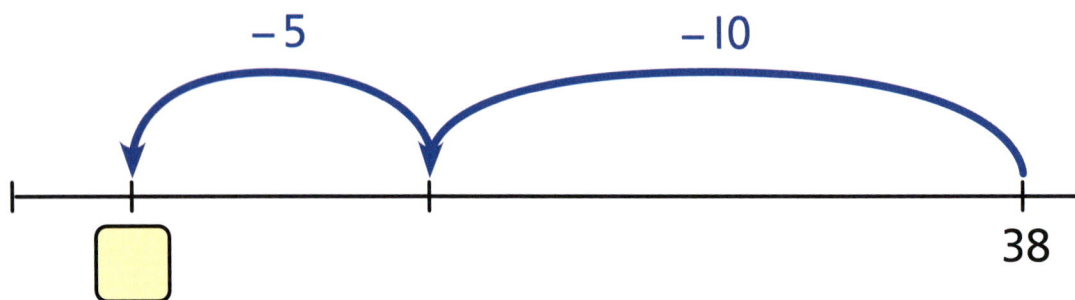

-5 -10

[ ]   38

2 a) Work out

44 – 13

44 – 31

b) What is the same?

What is different?

3 Compare and complete these methods.

Will

Anya

55 − 23 = ?
55 − 20 = 35
35 − 3 = 32

55 − 23 = ?
55 − 3 = 52
35 − 20 = 32

Try each method to solve the subtractions.

64 − 13 = ☐

48 − 35 = ☐

I will find which method I like best.

CHALLENGE

155

→ Practice book 2A p112

Subtract a 2-digit number from a 2-digit number – across 10

Discover

1 a) Kara has 24 strawberries. Will takes 10 strawberries.

How many strawberries are left in Kara's tray?

b) Asha takes another 5 strawberries.

How many strawberries are left in Kara's tray?

Share

a) There are 24 strawberries to start with.

Will takes 10 strawberries.

I used jumps on a number line.

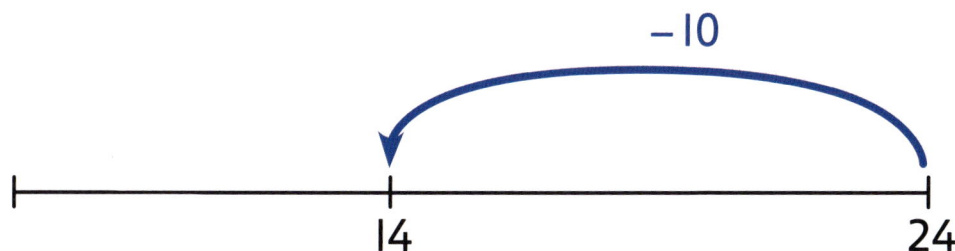

$24 - 10 = 14$

b) There are 14 strawberries left.

Asha takes 5 strawberries.

I have to subtract across 10. I need to do two more jumps.

To work out how many are left at the end you can do $24 - 15$.

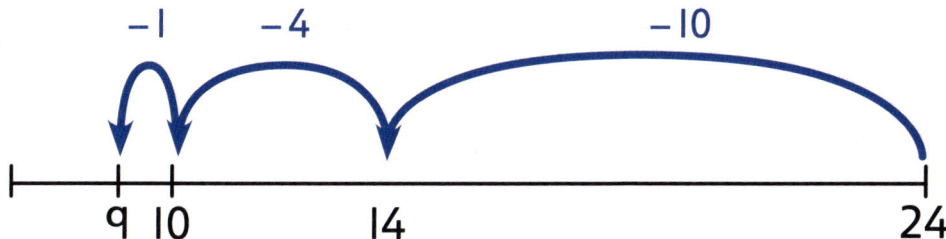

$24 - 10 - 5 = 9$

$24 - 15 = 9$

Think together

1 **a)** Work out 32 – 10.

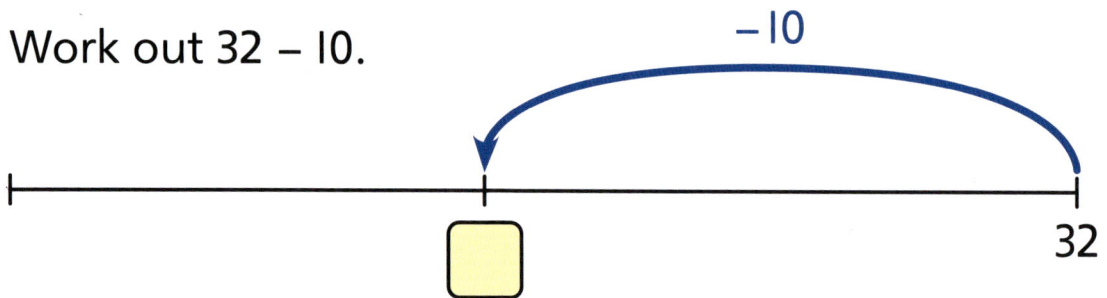

-10

32

b) Now work out 32 – 13.

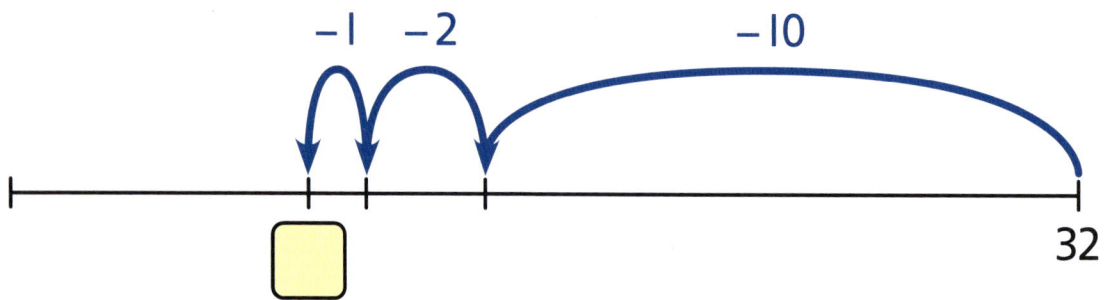

-1 -2 -10

32

2 **a)** Work out 52 – 15.

40   50 52

b) Now work out 52 – 25.

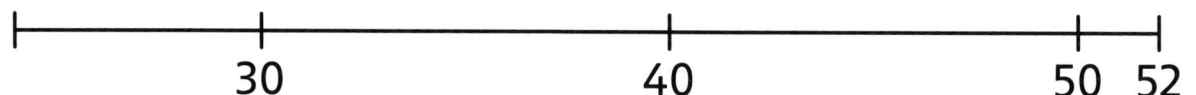

30   40   50 52

What is the same and what is different about the jumps you need?

3 **a)**

Kara

I know
11 – 7 = 4.

CHALLENGE

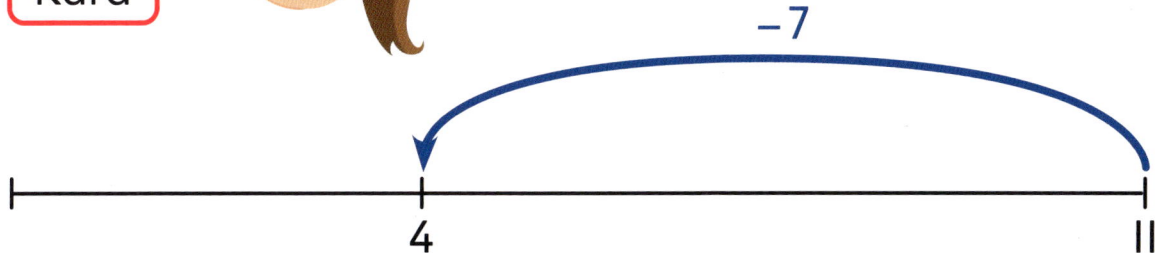

−7

4   11

Work out:

21 – 7 = ☐   31 – 7 = ☐   41 – 7 = ☐

51 – 7 = ☐   61 – 7 = ☐

b)

Maya

I know
31 – 17 = 14.

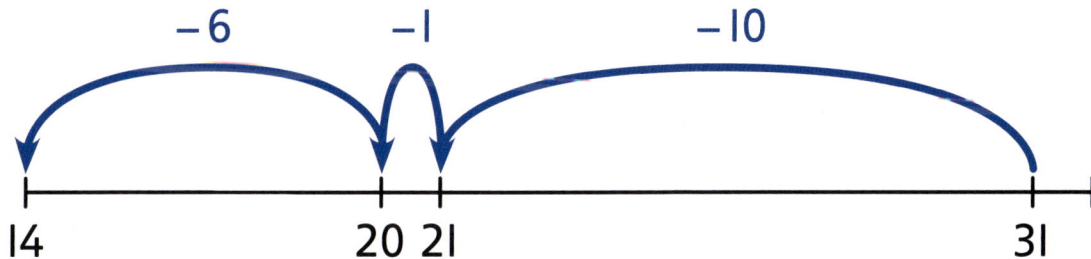

−6   −1   −10

14   20 21   31

Work out

51 – 17 = ☐   41 – 17 = ☐   81 – 17 = ☐

61 – 17 = ☐   21 – 17 = ☐

→ **Practice book 2A p115**

How many more? How many fewer?

Discover

1 **a)** How many more children are there in the back row?

   b) How many fewer children are there in the front row?

Share

a) This is a problem about 'finding the difference'.

```
 ├──┼──┼──┼──┼──┼──┼──┼──┼──┼──┤
 0  1  2  3  4  5  6  7  8  9  10
```

There are 2 more children in the back row.

> You can count on or count back to find the difference.

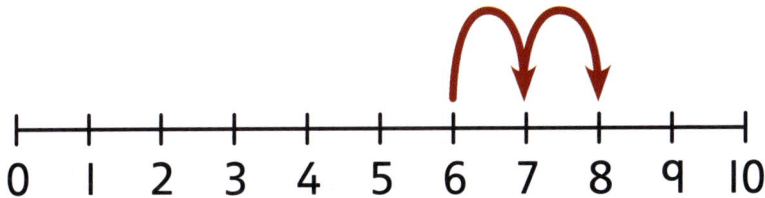

b)

```
 ├──┼──┼──┼──┼──┼──┼──┼──┼──┼──┤
 0  1  2  3  4  5  6  7  8  9  10
```

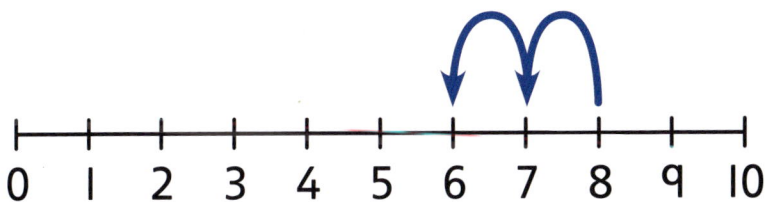

There are 2 fewer children in the front row.

8 is two more than 6.

6 is two less than 8.

The **difference** between 8 and 6 is 2.

Think together

1 Complete the statements.

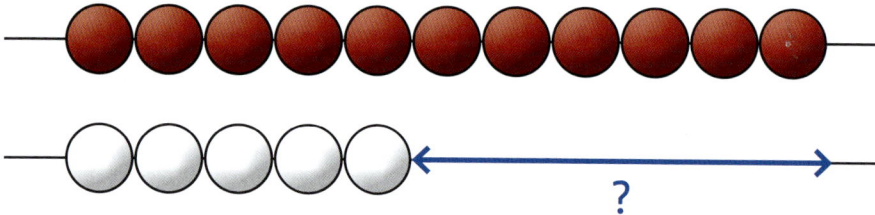

11 is ☐ more than 5.

5 is ☐ less than 11.

2 Complete the comparisons.

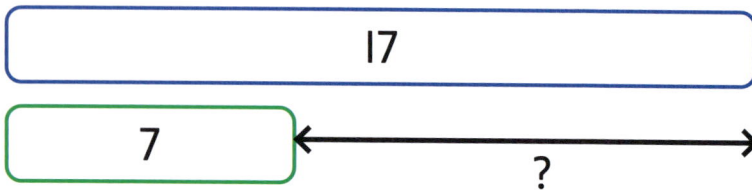

7 is _____ than 17.

17 is _____ than 7.

3 Find other pairs of numbers with a difference of 5.

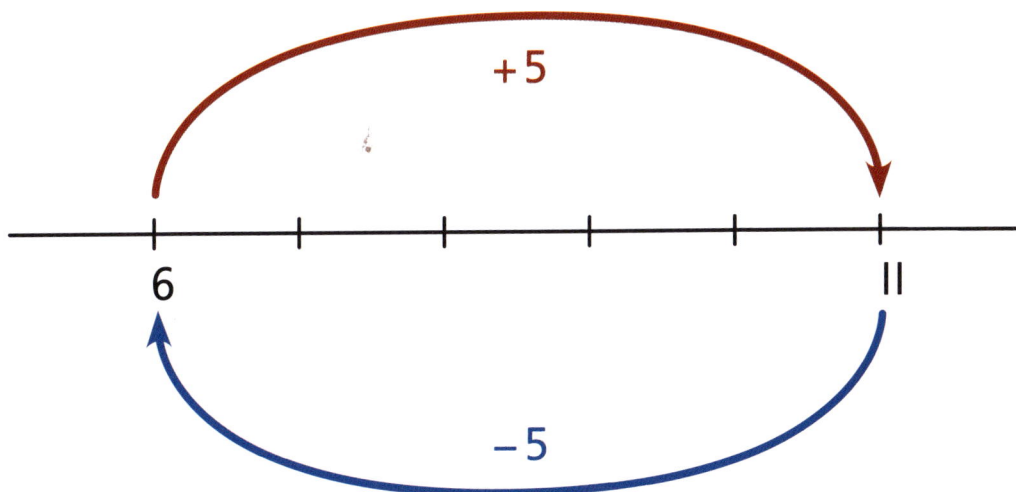

CHALLENGE

I found lots of pairs.
I noticed a pattern
in the 1s digits.

I am going to use a
number line to help me.

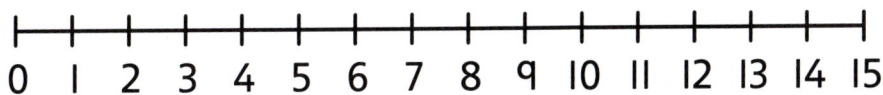

→ **Practice book 2A p118**

Subtraction – find the difference

Discover

1 a) How many years older is John than Sofia?

b) Solve 43 – 30 = ☐.

What do you notice?

Share

a) Sofia

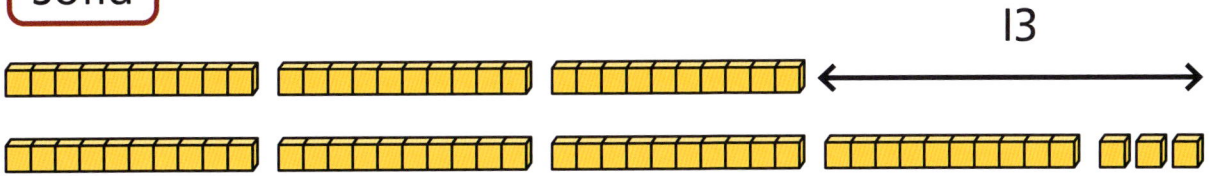

13

John

John is 13 years older than Sofia.

b)

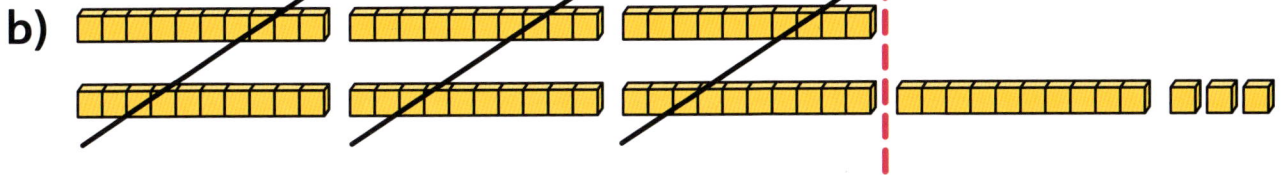

43 − 17 = 13

This is the difference between 43 and 30.

I will subtract to find the difference between the 2 numbers.

Think together

1 Complete the sentences.

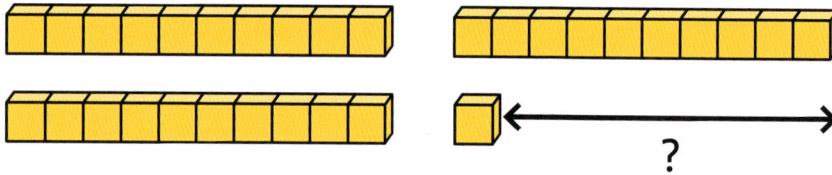

$20 - 11 = \boxed{}$

11 is $\boxed{}$ less than 20.

20 is $\boxed{}$ more than 11.

The difference between 11 and 20 is $\boxed{}$.

2 Complete the sentences.

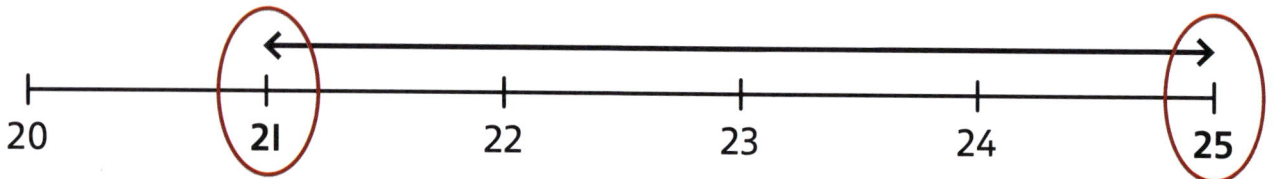

$$25 - 21 = \boxed{}$$

25 is $\boxed{}$ more than 21.

21 is $\boxed{}$ less than 25.

The difference between 21 and 25 is $\boxed{}$.

3 Discuss the two methods used by Maya and Kasim.

Which do you prefer?

35 – 32 = ☐

Maya

I took away 30 then 2.

I found the difference between 32 and 35.

Kasim

Solve these subtractions by finding the difference.

12 – 9 = ☐   65 – 11 = ☐

60 – 57 = ☐   81 – 79 = ☐

I wonder when this is a better method to solve subtractions.

167

→ Practice book 2A p121

Compare number sentences

Discover

"Make a tower of 11 cubes. Break it into parts."

1 a) Write an addition for each partition of 11.

b) Complete the number sentence.

$8 + 3 = 10 + \boxed{}$

Share

a) The children have partitioned 11 in different ways.

7 + 1 + 3 = 11

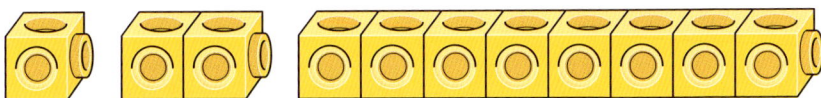

1 + 2 + 8 = 11

8 + 3 = 11

b)

8   3

10   1

8 + 3 = 10 + 1

First I used cubes to show 8 + 3.

Then I started with 10 and worked out how many more I needed.

169

Think together

1 Complete the number sentences. Use cubes to help you.

a) $6 + 2 = 5 + \boxed{}$

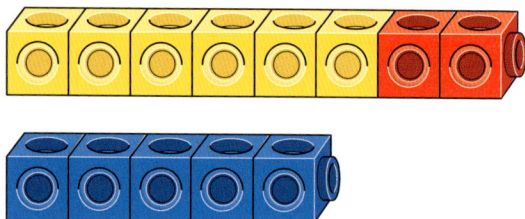

b) $6 + 2 = 4 + \boxed{}$

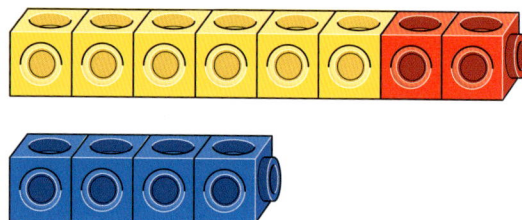

2 Choose < > or = to complete each number sentence.

a) $4 + 3 \bigcirc 4 + 2$

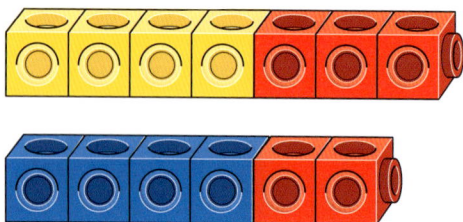

b) $8 - 2 \bigcirc 8 - 3$

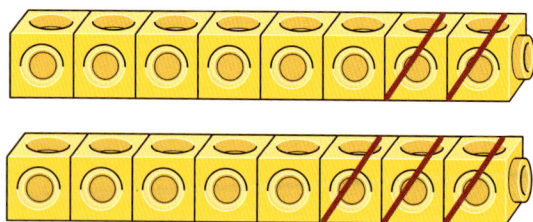

I can work out the symbol without calculating.

3 **a)** What numbers could go in each box?

CHALLENGE

$$6 + \boxed{} < 6 + 8$$

$$10 - 3 < 10 - \boxed{}$$

What are the smallest whole numbers that work?

> I'm going to try different numbers.

b) Complete these number sentences.

$$5 + 1 = 6 + \boxed{}$$

$$8 + 3 = 9 + \boxed{}$$

$$9 + 9 = 10 + \boxed{}$$

$$39 + 16 = 40 + \boxed{}$$

> I think there is a pattern for adding.

171

→ Practice book 2A p124

Missing number problems

Discover

a) Draw a part-whole model for this calculation.

b) What is Fred's missing number?

Share

a)

45
?   30

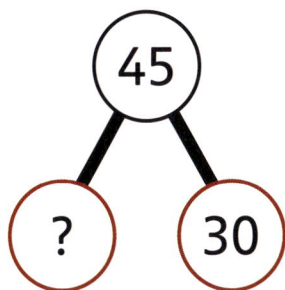

Remember.
Part + part = whole.

b) To work out the missing number you can do a subtraction.

Work out 45 – 30.

Remember.
Whole – part = part.

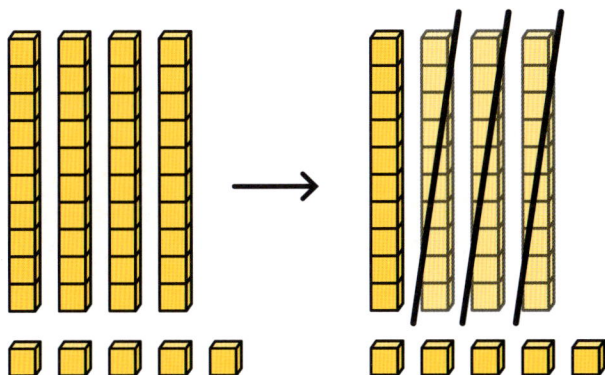

45 – 30 = 15

Fred's missing number is 15.

I used base 10 to work out the subtraction.
I know that
4 tens – 3 tens = 1 ten.
The 1s don't change.

Think together

1 **a)** What number is hidden?

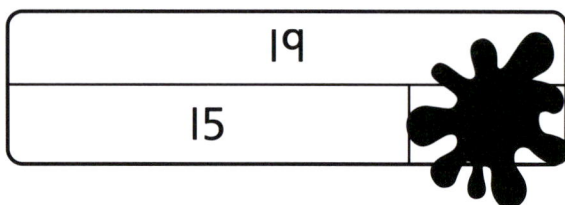

19	
15	✦

b) Work out the missing number calculation.

$$19 - \boxed{} = 15$$

2 Calculate the missing numbers.

$$5 + \bigstar = 25$$

$$25 - \text{☁} = 24$$

$$\triangle + \triangle = 10.$$

I think the two triangles are the same number.

3 **a)** What number is each shape?

CHALLENGE

$$\text{(green diamond)} + 7 = 9$$

$$\text{(orange triangle)} - 9 = 7$$

$$9 = \text{(blue cloud)} - 7$$

$$\text{(red heart)} = 9 - 7$$

> I will decide if each missing number is missing the whole or the part.

b) Find the value of each of the shapes.

Do all the rows and columns add up to 20?

(red circle)	(red circle)	10	**20**
(red circle)	(orange triangle)	6	**20**
(orange triangle)	(blue heart)	4	**20**
?	?	**20**	

→ Practice book 2A p127

Mixed addition and subtraction

Discover

1 **a)** Mr Dean has 57 stickers. He buys 30 more.

How many does he have altogether?

b) Mr Dean then puts 1 sticker in each book.

There are 45 books.

How many stickers are left?

Share

I know part + part = whole, and whole − part = part.

I have used a bar model to represent this. It helps me to see what is going on.

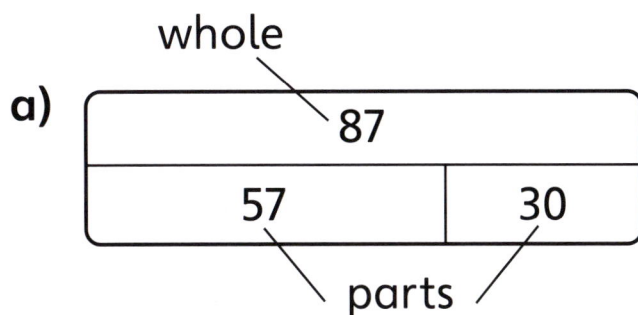

whole

a)

87	
57	30

parts

$57 + 30 = 87$

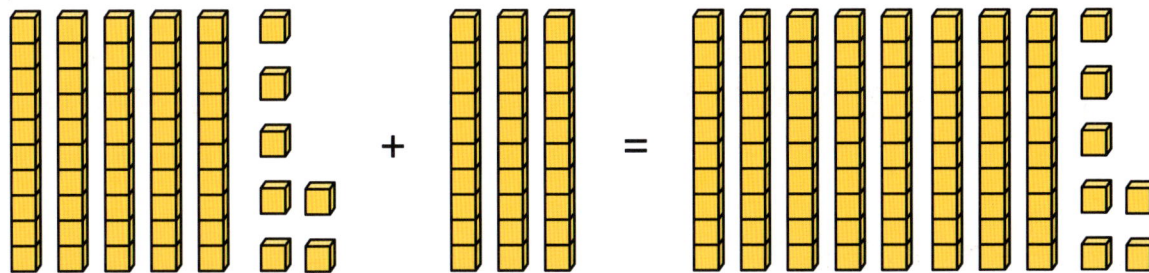

Mr Dean has 87 stickers.

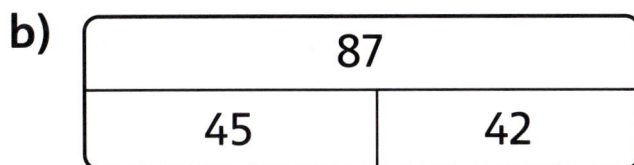

b)

87	
45	42

$87 - 45 = 42$

Mr Dean has 42 stickers left.

Think together

1 There are 45 pupils in total.

27 have school dinners. The rest have a packed lunch.

How many pupils have a packed lunch?

45	
27	?

$45 \bigcirc 27 = \square$

$\square$ pupils have a packed lunch.

2 There are 35 yellow stickers and 16 blue stickers.

How many stickers are there altogether?

?	
?	?

$35 \bigcirc 16 = \square$

There are $\square$ stickers altogether.

3 Mrs Bell uses 7 blue stickers, 5 red stickers and 9 yellow stickers.

CHALLENGE

How many stickers does she use altogether?

?		
?	?	?

☐ ○ ☐ ○ ☐ = ☐

We need to work out the whole.

I think there are 3 parts. Is that possible?

Mrs Bell uses ☐ stickers altogether.

→ **Practice book 2A p130**

Two-step problems

Discover

1 **a)** How many marbles are there in Amy's and Kasim's pots altogether?

b) Work out the difference between the numbers of marbles in Kat's and Ben's pots.

Share

a)

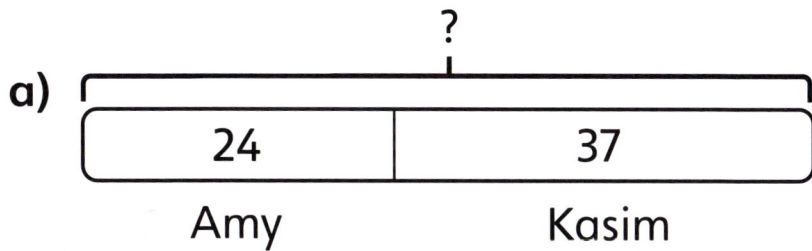

I used a number line to work out the answers.

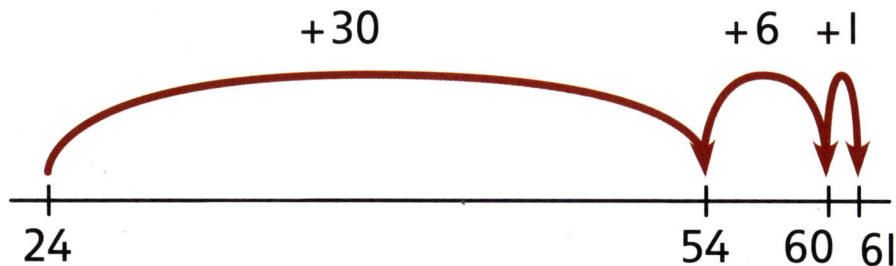

$24 + 37 = 61$

There are 61 marbles in Amy's and Kasim's pots altogether.

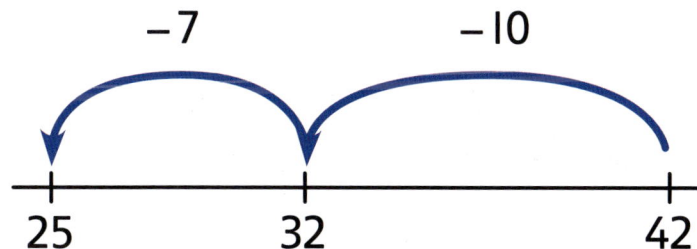

b) Kat 42

Ben 17 ?

$42 - 17 = 25$

There are 25 more marbles in Kat's pot than in Ben's pot.

Think together

Ben   Kat   Amy   Kasim   Maya

1 How many marbles are there in Ben's and Amy's pots altogether?

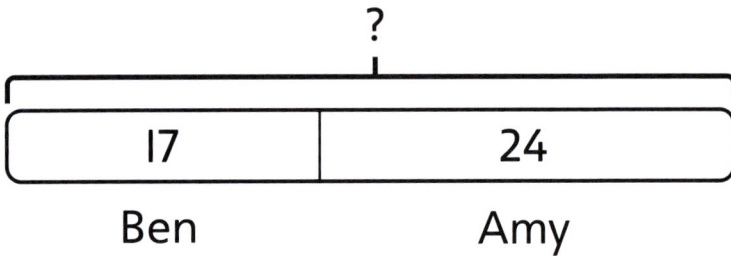

?

| 17 | 24 |

Ben   Amy

17 ◯ 24 = ▢

2 Maya's pot has 15 more marbles in it than Kat's pot.

How many marbles are in Maya's pot?

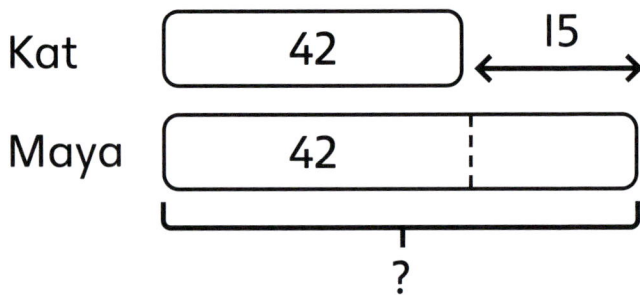

Kat | 42 | ← 15 →

Maya | 42 | |

?

182

3 19 more marbles are added to Ben's pot.

How many more marbles are there in Ben's pot than in Amy's pot now?

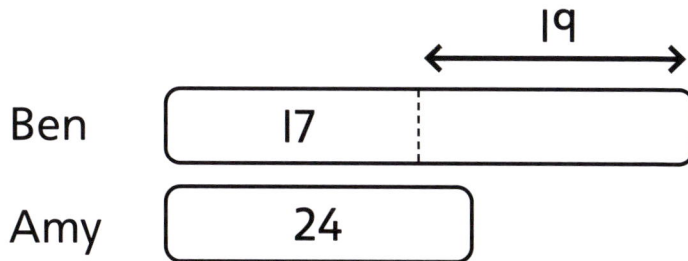

CHALLENGE

Ben | 17 | ← 19 →

Amy | 24 |

I can see that there are two parts to this question.

I will draw out the information I know, to make it easier!

→ Practice book 2A p133

End of unit check

> Your teacher will ask you these questions.

1 How many altogether?

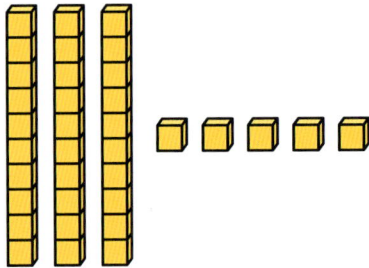

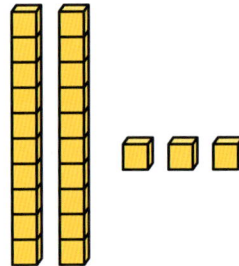

| A 85 | B 13 | C 58 | D 40 |

2 What is 10 more than 37?

| A 27 | B 38 | C 47 | D 57 |

3 Work out 65 – 20.

65	
20	

| A 40 | B 45 | C 63 | D 85 |

4 Which calculation finds the missing number?

$$17 + \boxed{} = 52$$

A 17 + 52   **B** 52 + 17   **C** 17 – 52   **D** 52 – 17

5 There are 95 children in a class.

One teacher has 42 strawberries. Another teacher has 25 strawberries.

How many more do they need so each child can have one strawberry?

A 77   **B** 53   **C** 88   **D** 28

Think!

Circle the odd one out.

Prove it.

37	28

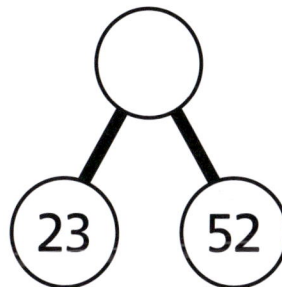

$$\boxed{} = 46 + 19$$

These words will help you.

ones   tens   equals

add   subtract

185

→ Practice book 2A p136

Unit 4
Properties of shapes

In this unit we will …
- ⚡ Recognise 2D and 3D shapes
- ⚡ Count the sides and vertices on 2D shapes
- ⚡ Learn about symmetry
- ⚡ Count the faces, edges and vertices on 3D shapes
- ⚡ Sort 2D and 3D shapes

How are these shapes similar? How are they different?

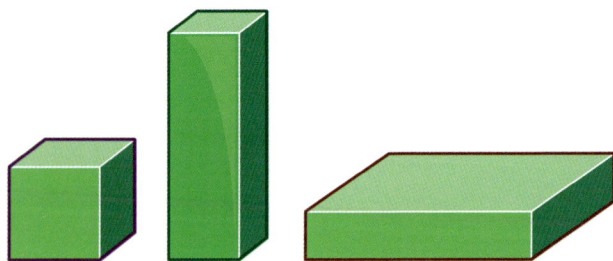

We need lots of words to describe 2D and 3D shapes. Do you know any of these words?

pentagon   polygon   prism

quadrilateral   hexagon   hemisphere

symmetry   symmetrical   vertex

vertices   edge   side   face

line of symmetry   curved surface

Do you remember what these shapes are called?

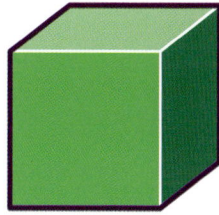

Recognise 2D and 3D shapes

Discover

1 a) Which picture did Mia make?

b) Which picture did Sunil make?

Share

a) Mia's picture has 2 squares.

Which picture has 2 squares?

I think a square looks like this ☐.

This is Mia's picture.

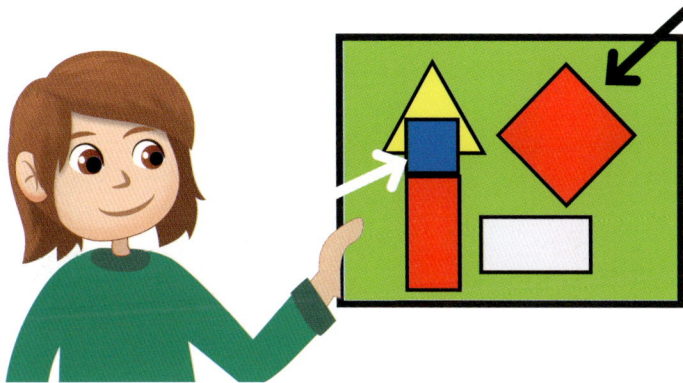

Rectangles and squares are **quadrilaterals** because they have 4 **sides**.

b) This is Sunil's picture.

Think together

1 How many rectangles are there in this picture?

I can name other shapes in the picture too.

2 Name the 3D shapes.

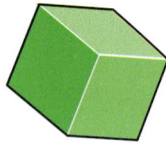

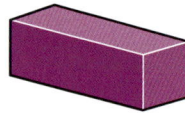

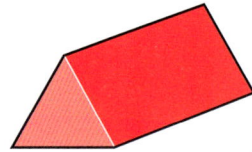

Which 3D shapes could you use to print the 2D shapes in the pictures?

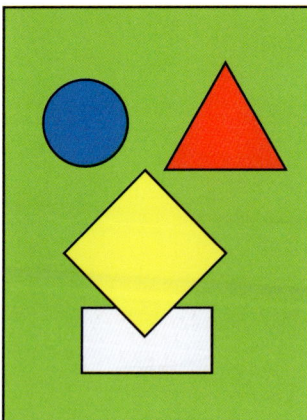

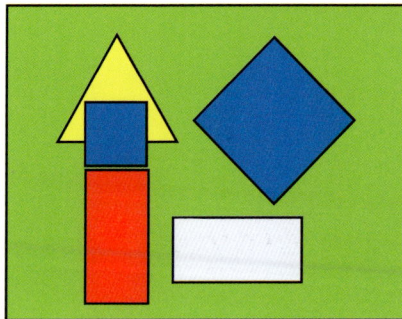

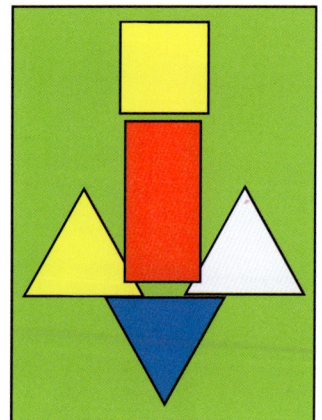

CHALLENGE

3 Ben draws around the base of a cuboid to make a rectangle.

Which 2D shapes can you draw using these 3D shapes?

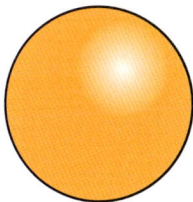

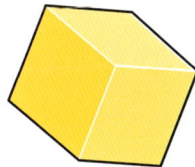

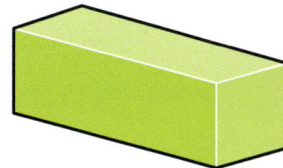

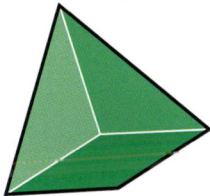

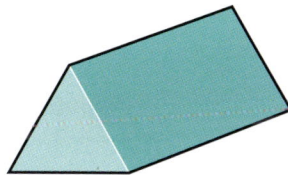

I will draw around all of these shapes.

191

→ Practice book 2A p138

Count sides on 2D shapes

Discover

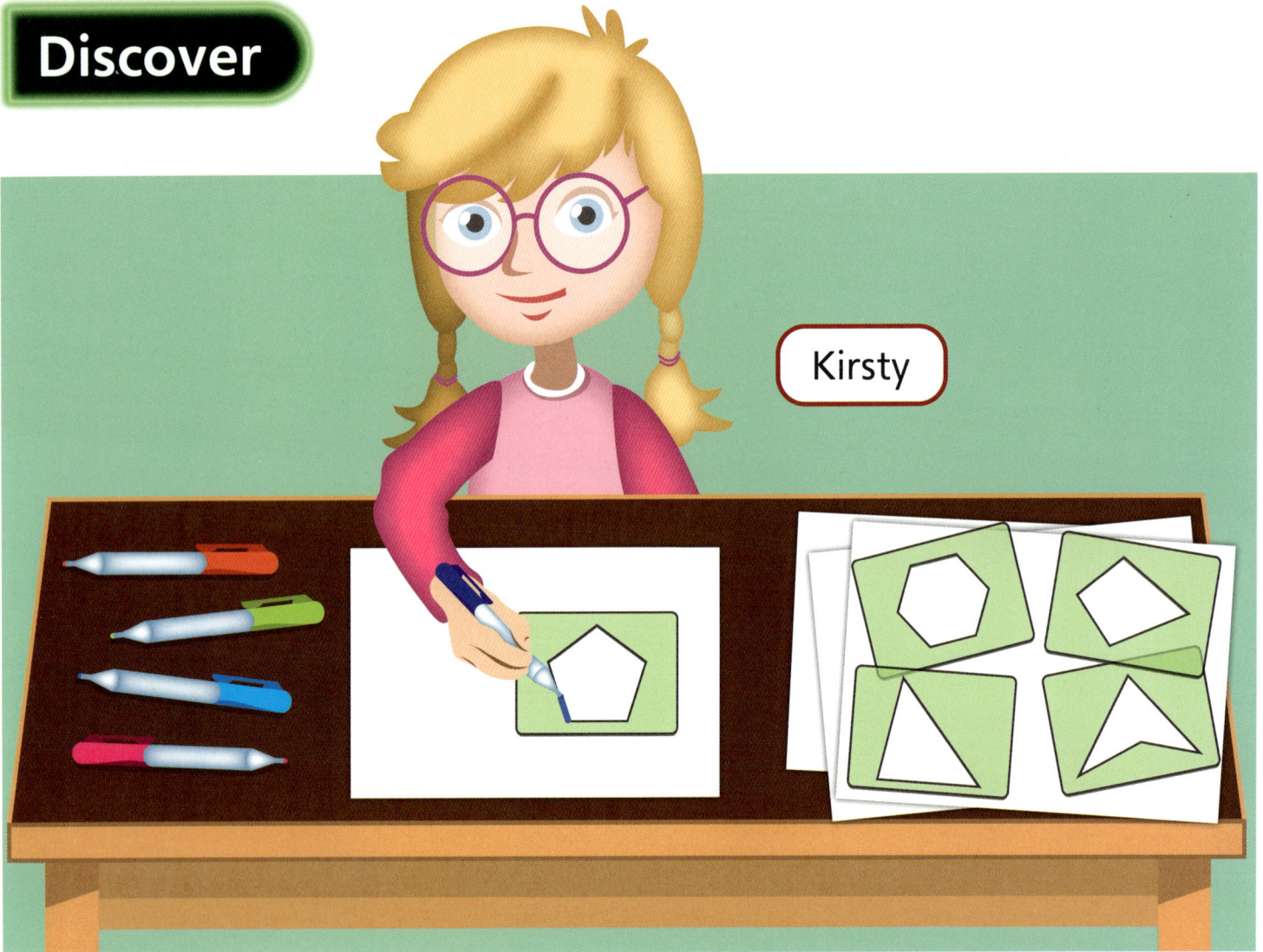

Kirsty

1 **a)** Kirsty wants to use a different colour for each side of the shape ⬠.

How many pens will she use?

b) Kirsty has 5 different colour pens.

Does she have enough pens to draw the sides of each shape in a different colour?

Share

a)

A side is a straight line that joins 2 corners of a 2D shape.

I counted all sides.

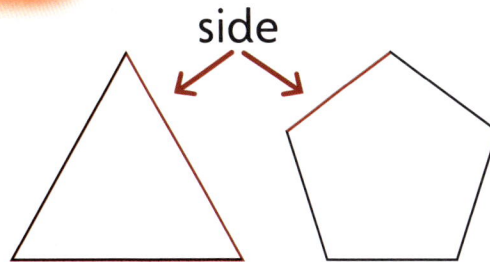

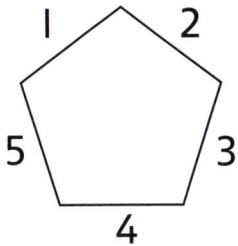

side

This shape has 5 sides.

A shape with 5 sides is called a **pentagon**.

Kirsty will use 5 different coloured pens for a pentagon.

b) Kirsty has 5 different colour pens.

She can draw these shapes.

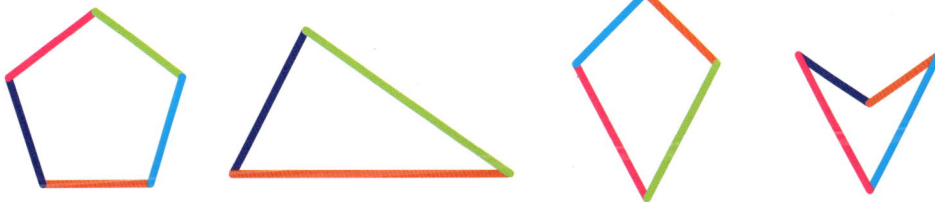

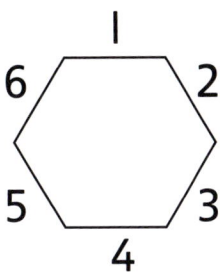

A ⬡ has 6 sides.

A shape with 6 sides is called a **hexagon**.

Kirsty does not have enough pens to draw each side of a hexagon in a different colour.

Think together

1

I wonder if there are other quadrilaterals.

Kat only wants to draw quadrilateral shapes.

Which shapes should she draw?

2 Milo is making shapes using sticks.

How many sides does each shape have?

3 Count the sides of each shape.

How many of the shapes are quadrilaterals?

CHALLENGE

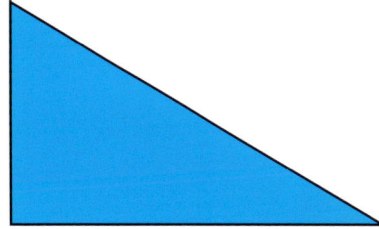

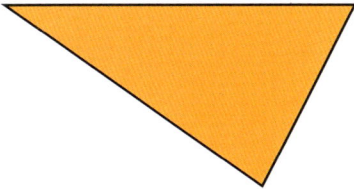

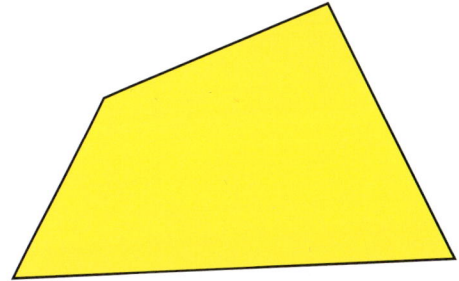

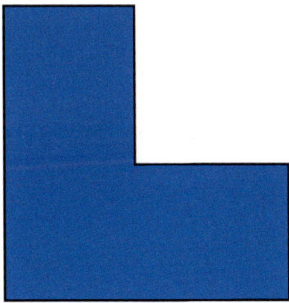

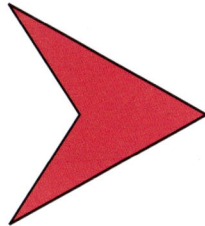

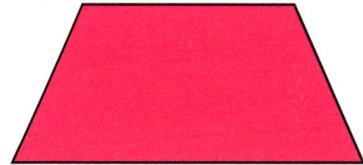

I will also try to remember the special names for some of the shapes.

195

→ Practice book 2A p141

Count vertices on 2D shapes

Discover

1 **a)** How many fingers do the children need to make a square?

How many fingers do they need for a pentagon?

b) How many different shapes can you make using 3 fingers?

Share

a) A square needs 4 fingers because it has 4 corners.

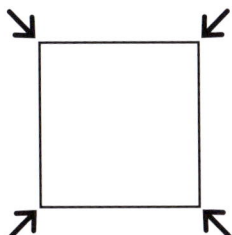

The accurate name for a corner is a **vertex**. The plural is **vertices**.

I counted how many vertices a pentagon has.

There are 5 vertices on a pentagon so the children need to use 5 fingers.

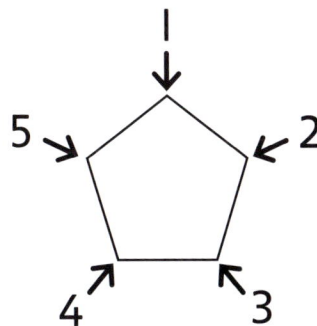

b)

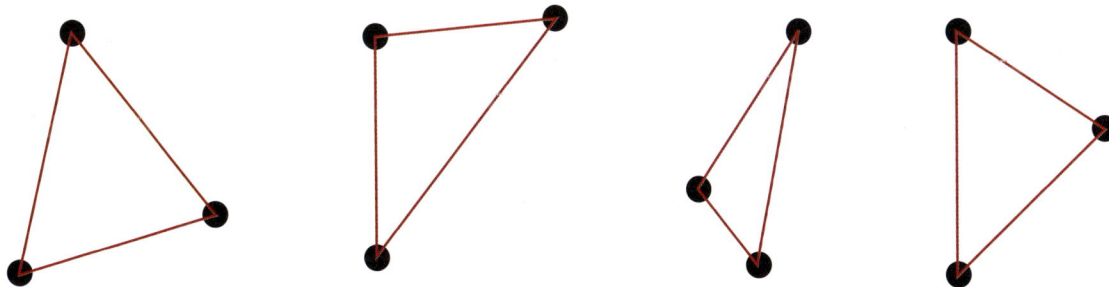

The only shape you can make with 3 fingers is a triangle. It has 3 vertices.

Think together

1 Count the number of vertices on each shape.

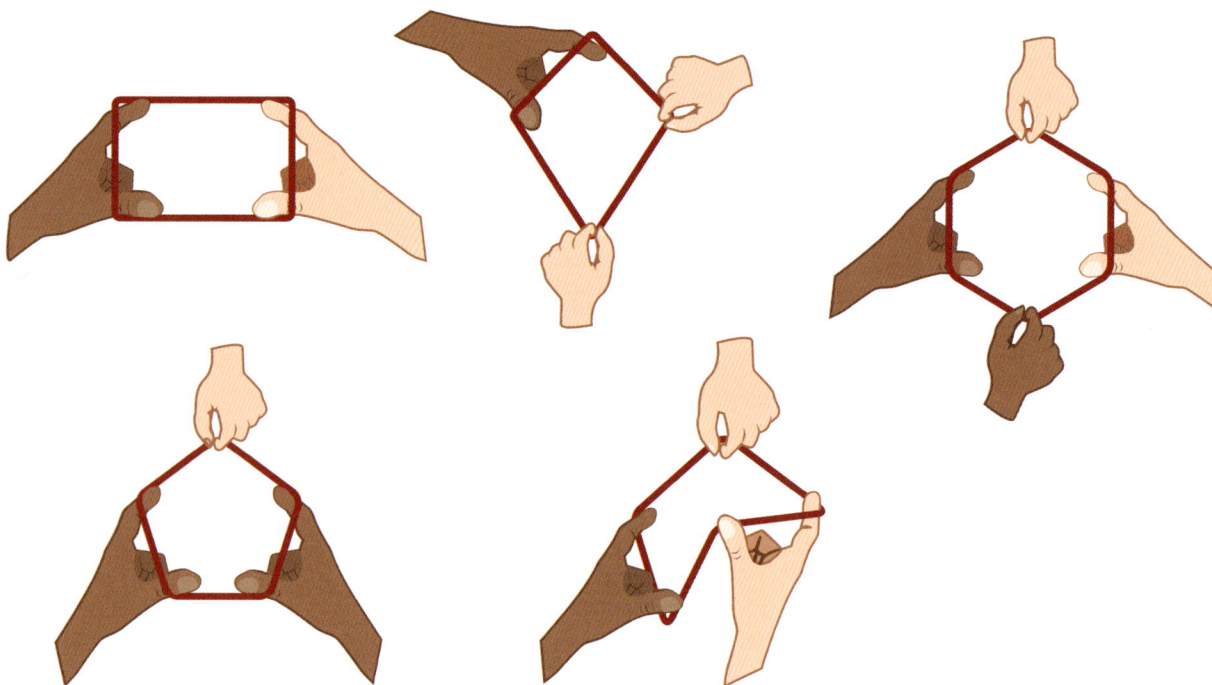

2 Count the number of vertices on each shape.

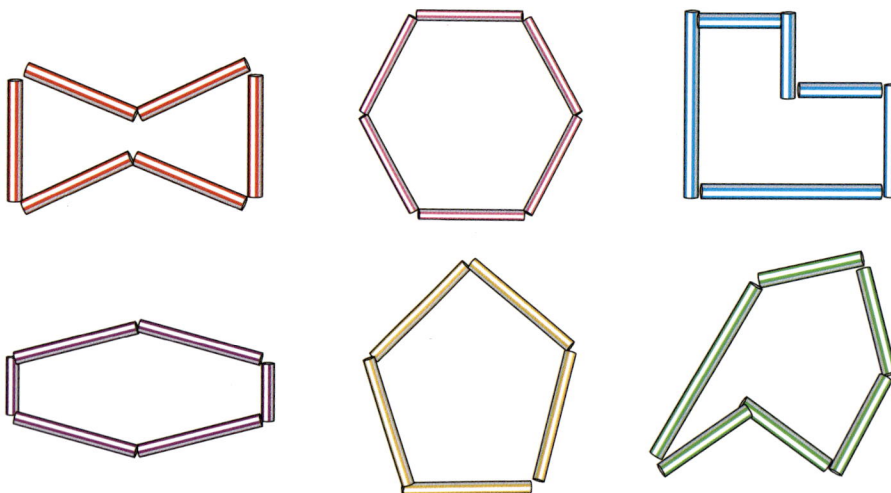

3

1

3   2

triangle

1   2

3

5   4

pentagon

CHALLENGE

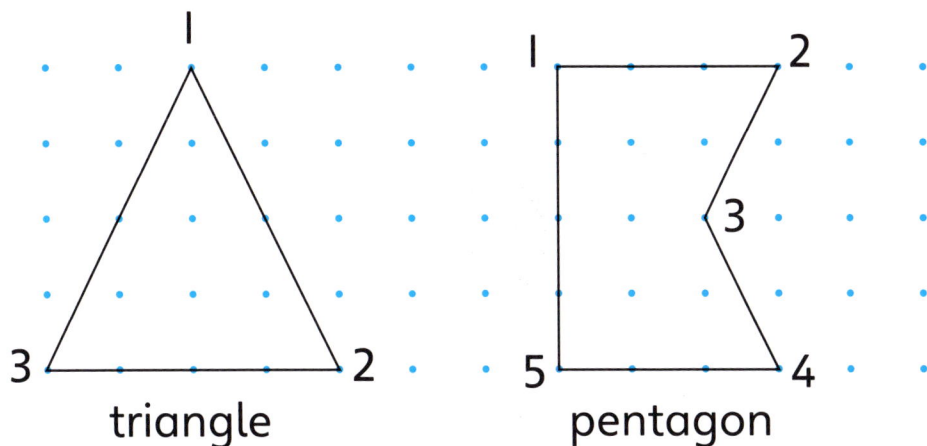

A triangle has 3 sides and 3 vertices. A pentagon has 5 sides and 5 vertices.

Count the number of sides and vertices of these shapes.

A

B

C

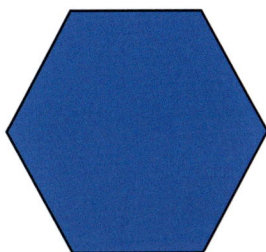

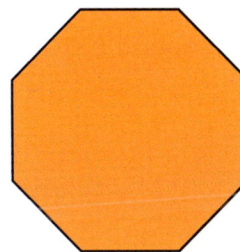

☐ sides
☐ vertices

☐ sides
☐ vertices

☐ sides
☐ vertices

What do you notice?

199

→ Practice book 2A p144

Draw 2D shapes

Discover

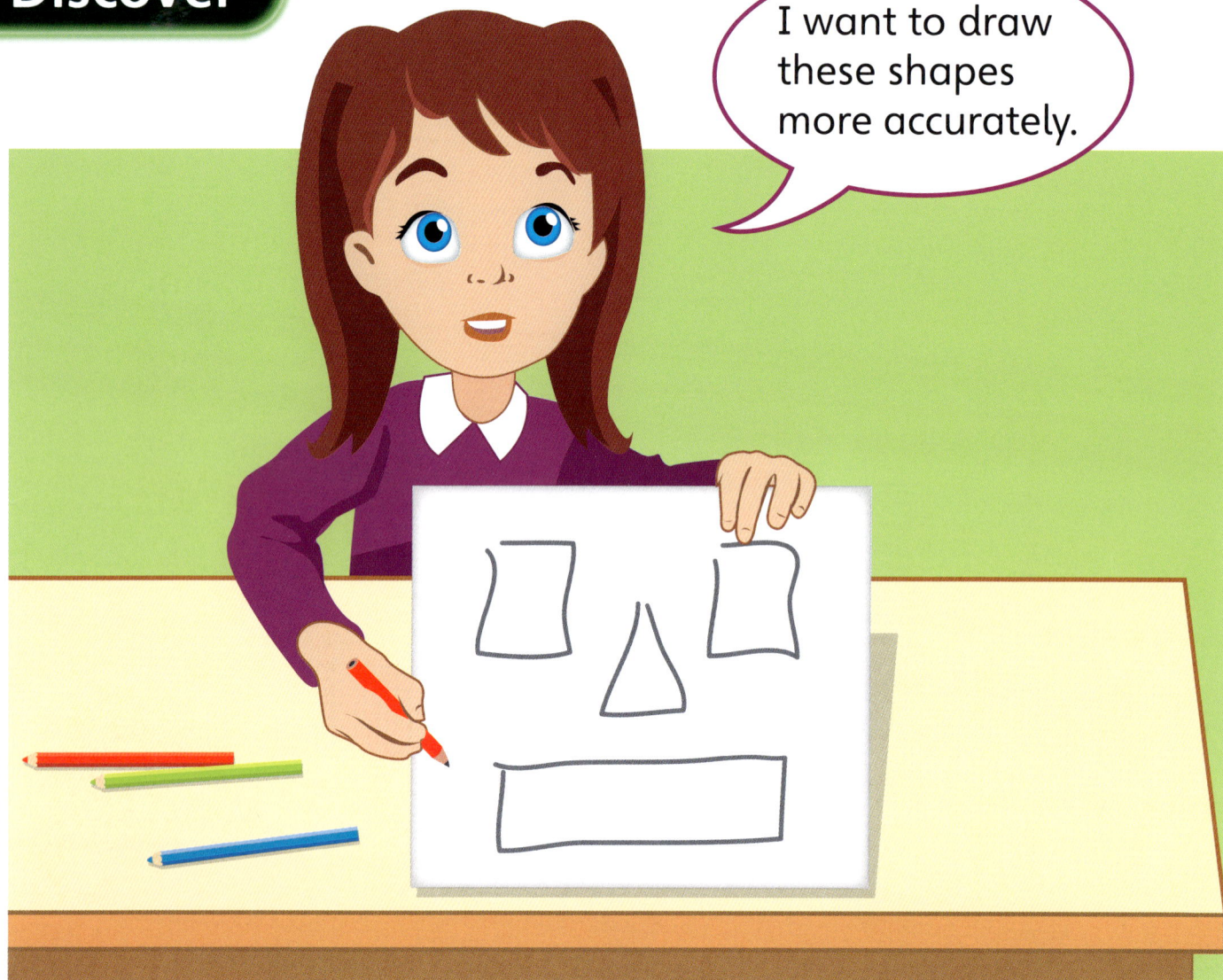

I want to draw these shapes more accurately.

1 a) Draw a square accurately.

b) Draw a triangle accurately.

Share

a) To draw a square, you need 4 corners.

> I used squared paper and a ruler to help.

Work out where the corners should go.

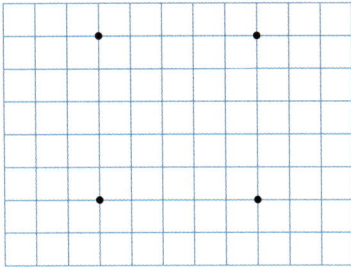

Line up 2 dots with a ruler.

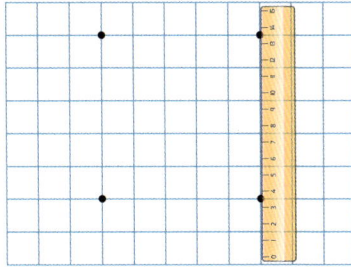

Draw a line between the dots.

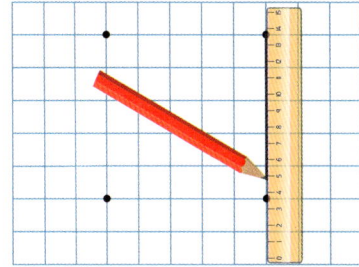

> I used a ruler and drew all 4 sides in the same way.

b) You need 3 dots to draw a triangle.

Line up 2 dots with a ruler. Draw a line between the dots. Draw each side in this way.

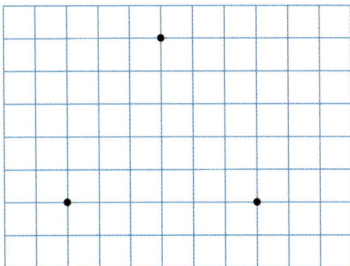

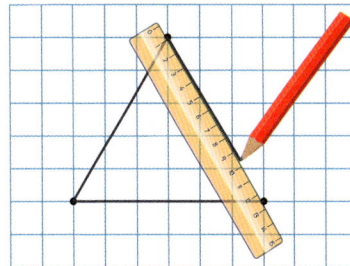

Think together

You will need to add more dots.

1 Copy these dots on squared paper.

Use them to draw two different rectangles.

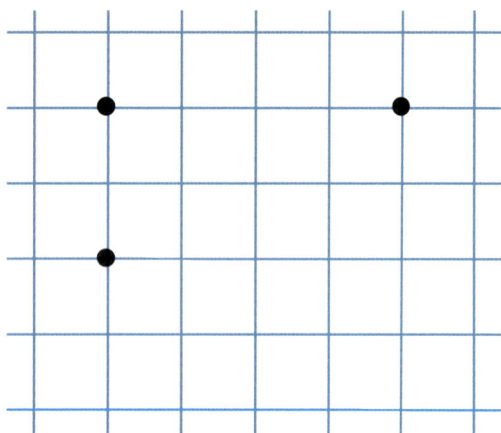

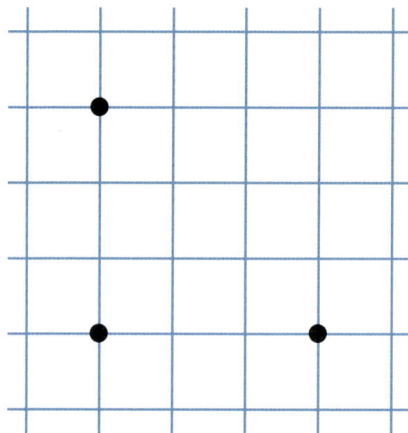

2 Copy these triangles.

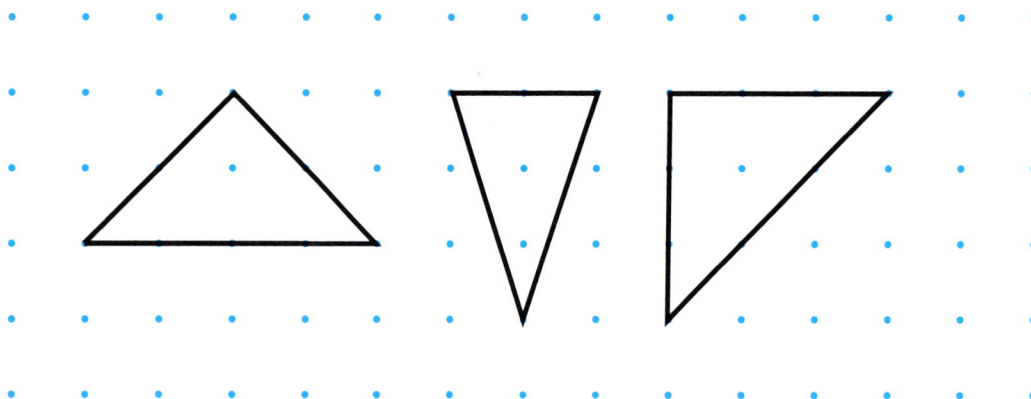

CHALLENGE

3 **a)** The dots in these shapes have been joined together.

Copy the shapes accurately on squared paper.

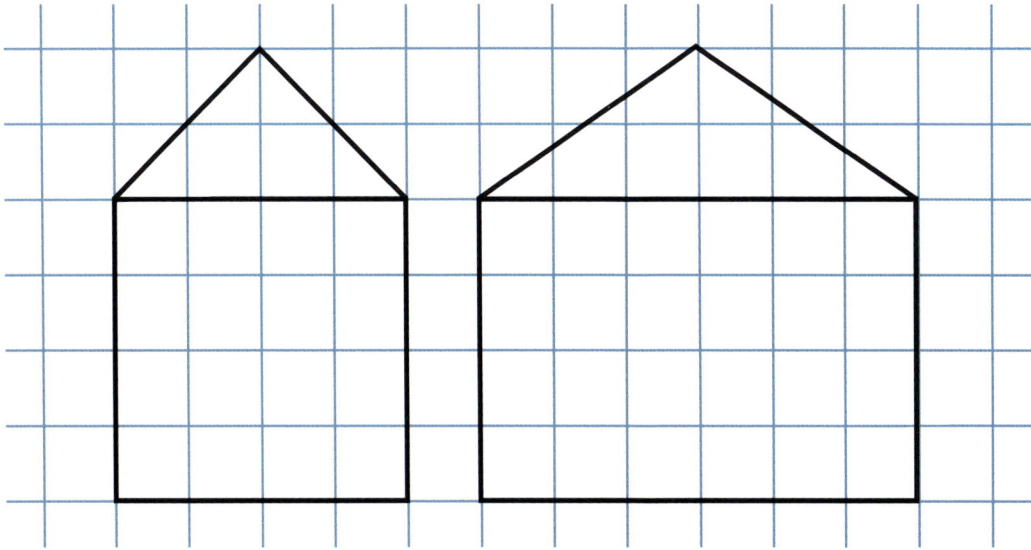

b) Now draw these shapes on plain paper.

I will use a ruler and pencil.

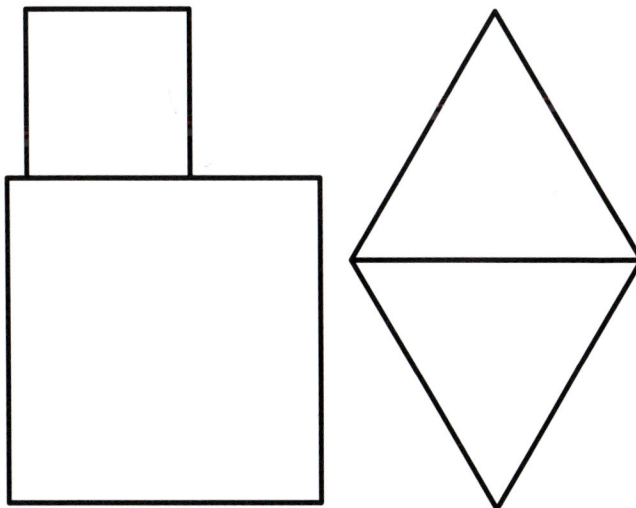

→ **Practice book 2A p147**

Lines of symmetry on shapes

Discover

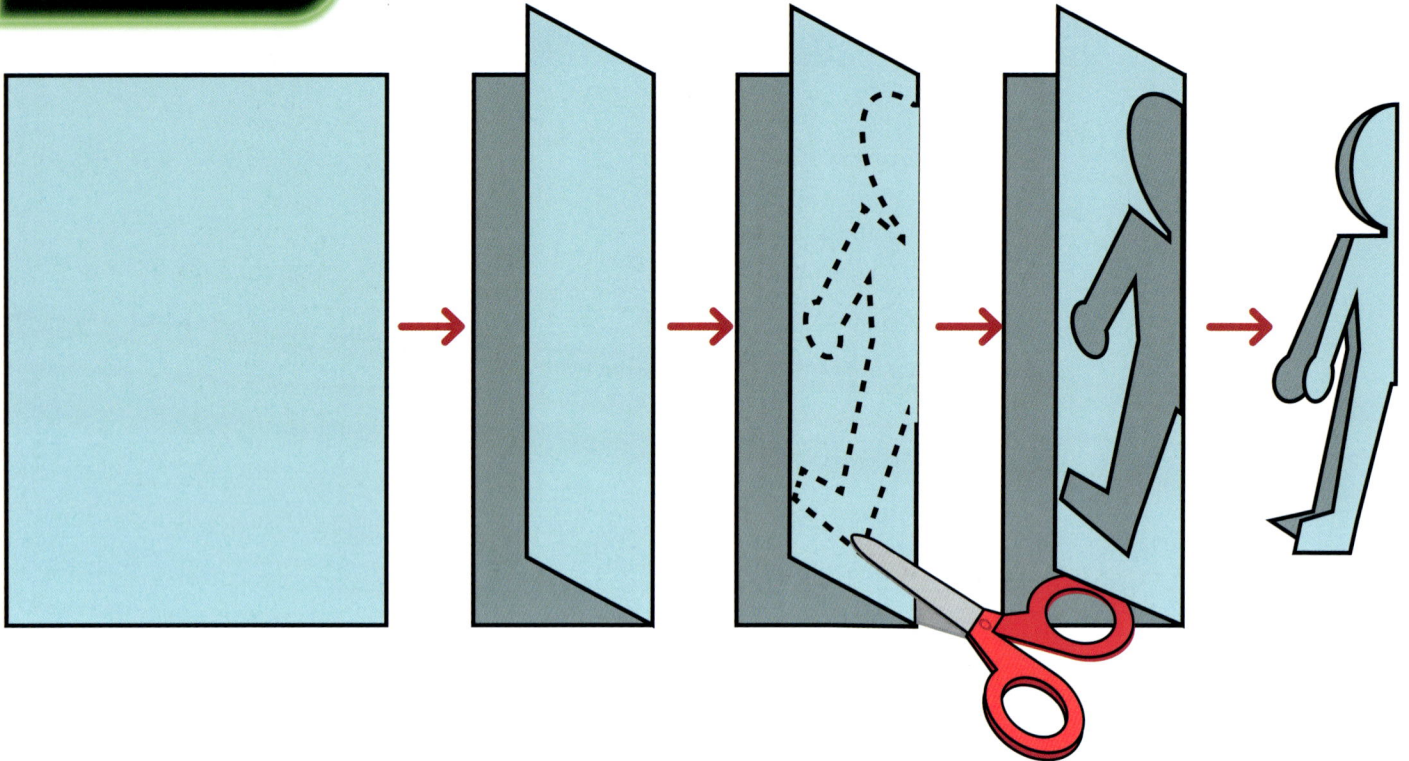

1 **a)** Describe what the cut-out shape will look like when it is unfolded.

b) What will this shape look like when it is unfolded?

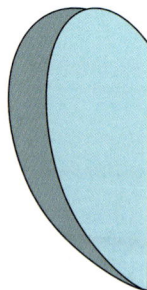

Share

a) The shape will look like a person when it is unfolded.

The line between the two halves is called the **line of symmetry**.

When the paper is folded on the line of symmetry, the two parts match exactly.

The shape is **symmetrical**.

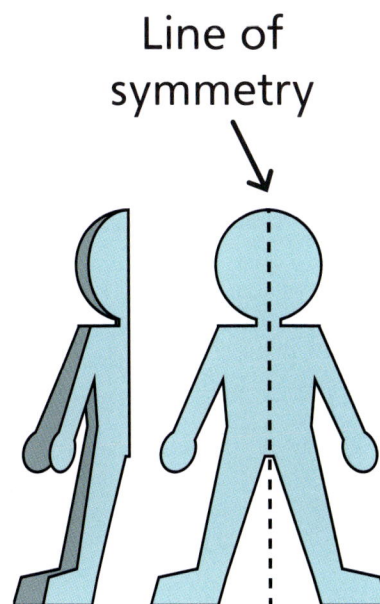

Line of symmetry

b) This shape is symmetrical too.

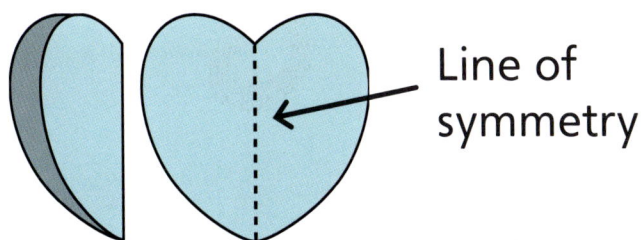

Line of symmetry

The shape will look like a heart when it is unfolded.

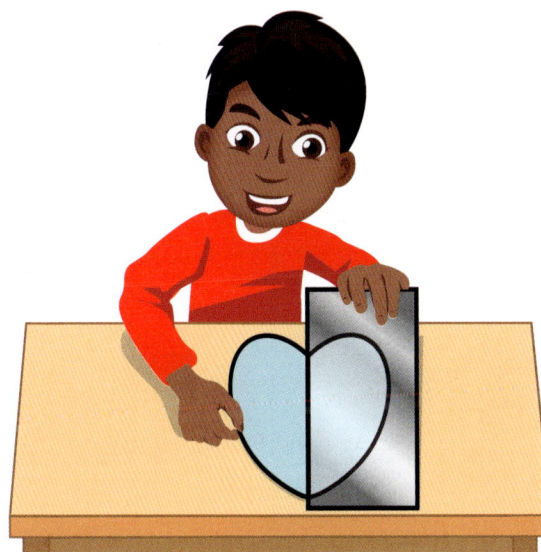

You can use a mirror to see that the shape is symmetrical.

Think together

1 What will these shapes look like when they are unfolded?

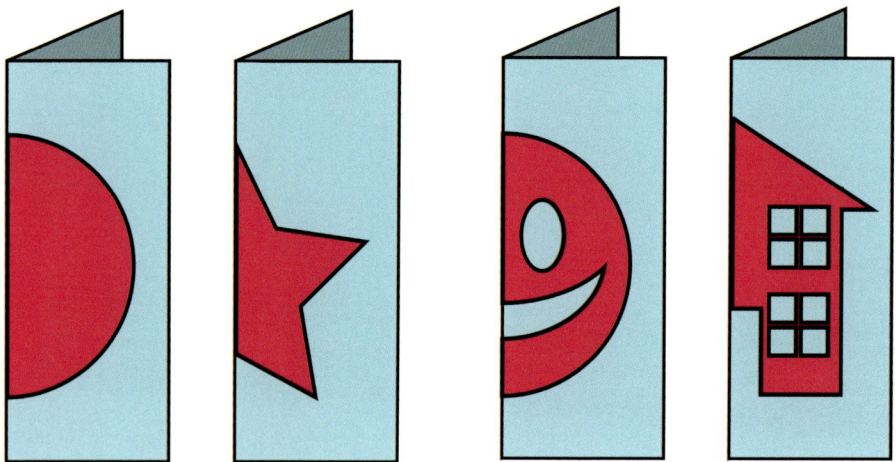

2 Complete the symmetrical shapes.

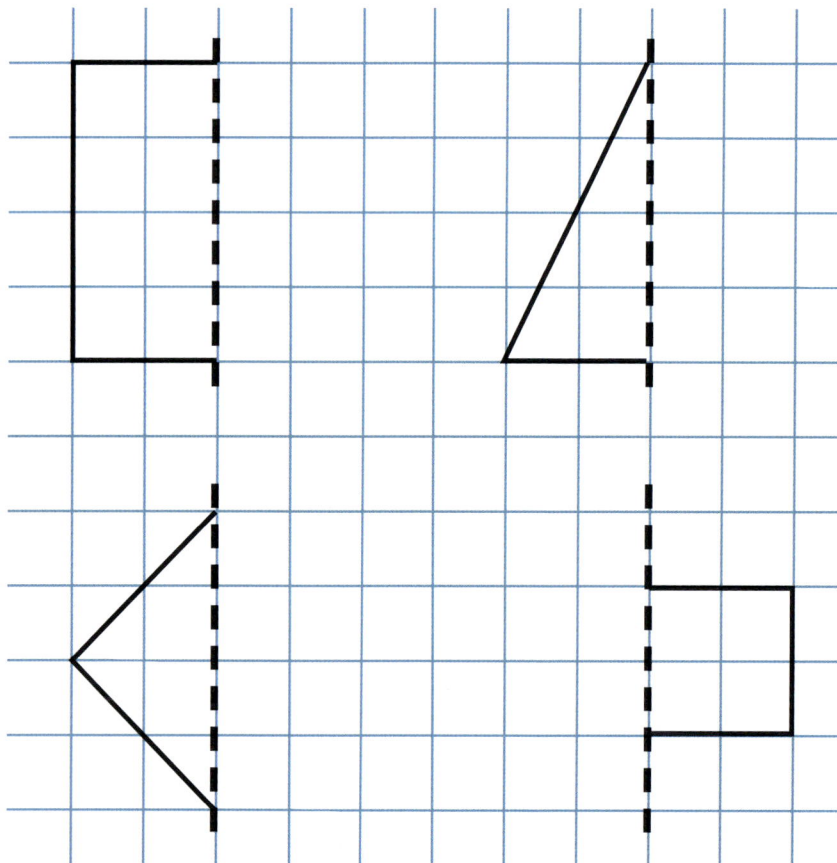

I will check using a mirror.

3 Which lines of symmetry are correct?

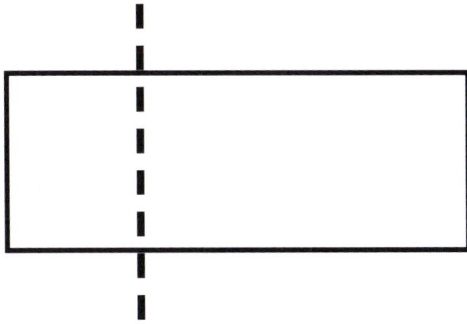

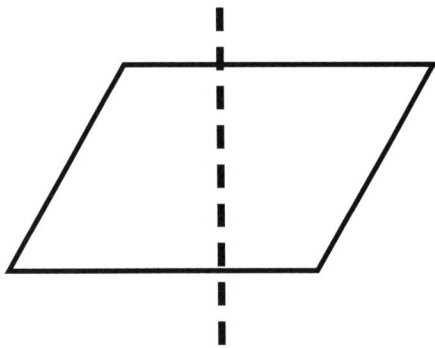

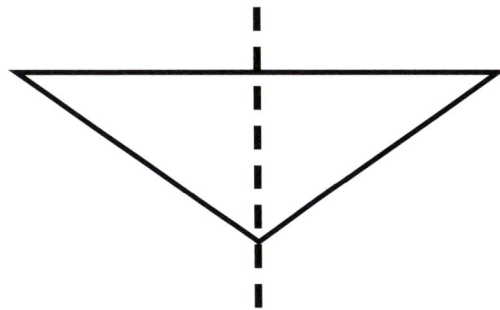

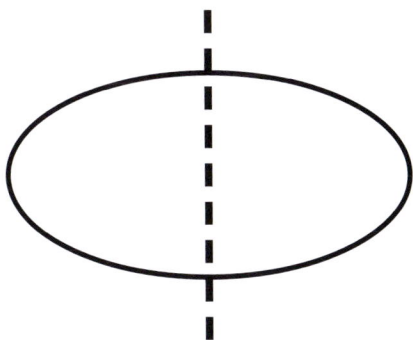

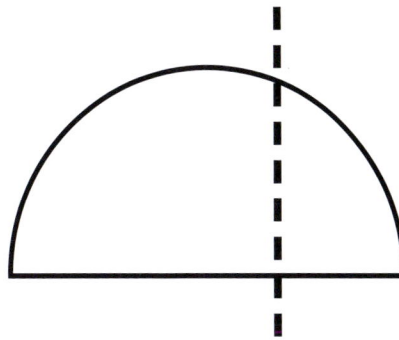

CHALLENGE

I can make my own shape with a line of symmetry.

207

→ Practice book 2A p150

Sort 2D shapes

Discover

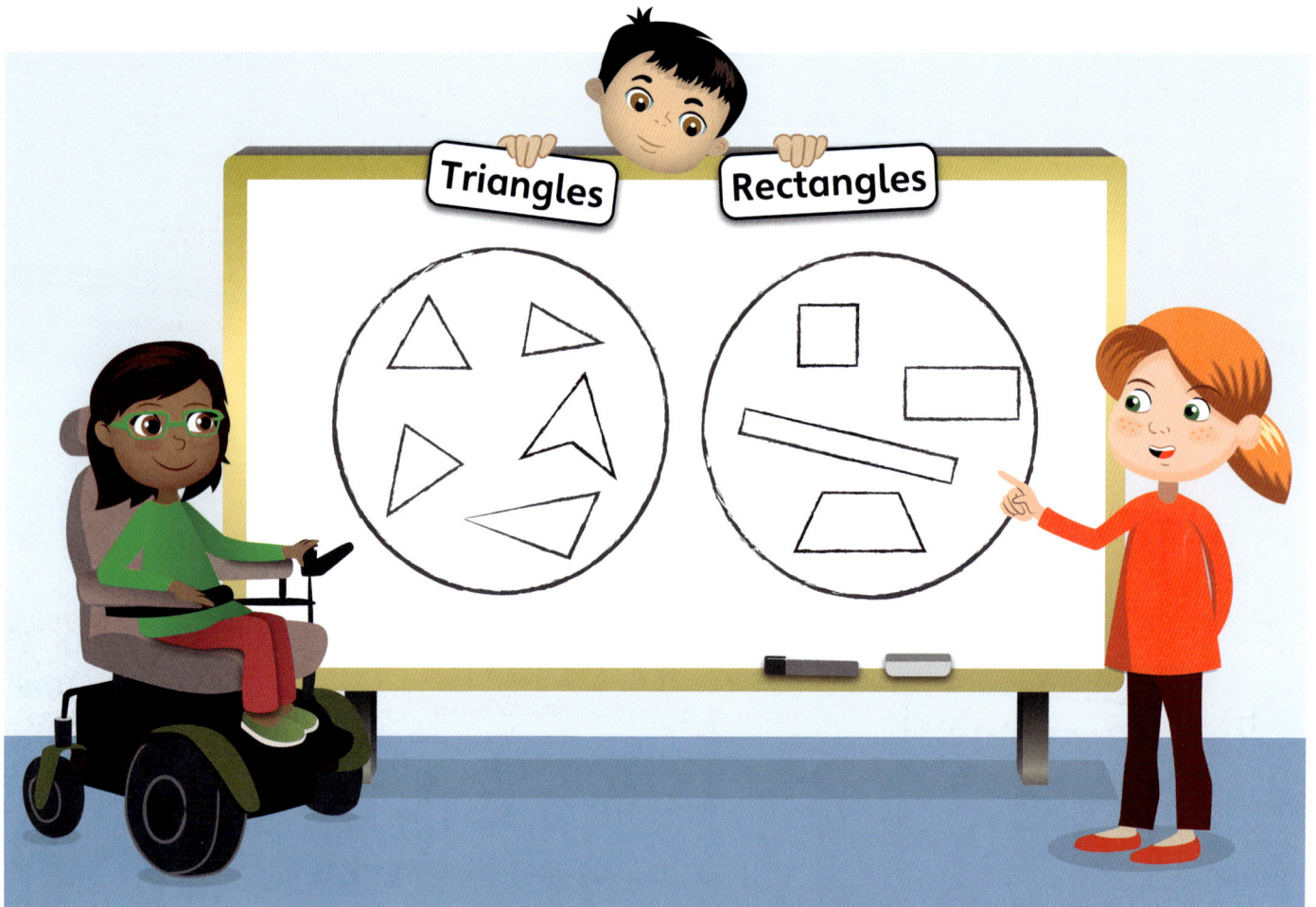

1 **a)** Find the mistake in the 'Triangles' sorting circle.

b) Find the mistake in the 'Rectangles' sorting circle.

Share

a)

Triangles

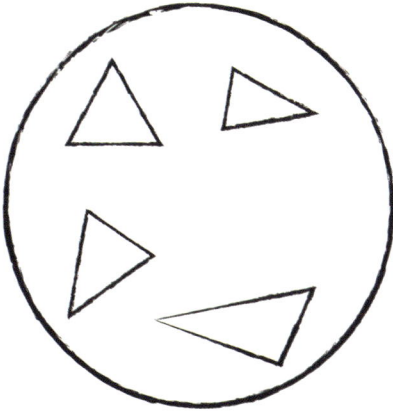

A triangle must have:
- Exactly 3 straight sides
- Exactly 3 corners.

This shape is not a triangle.

It has 4 sides.

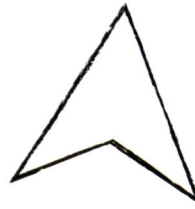

b)

Rectangles

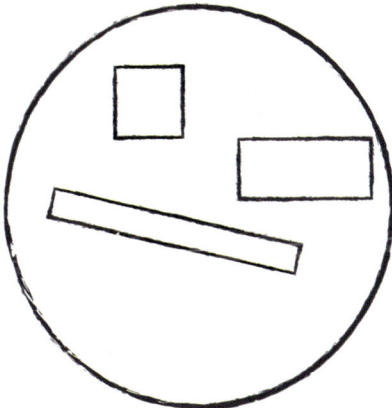

I think a square must be a special kind of rectangle.

This shape is not a rectangle.

It has 2 opposite sides of different lengths.

Think together

1 What labels could go on these boxes?

I think a **polygon** is a 2D shape with straight sides.

I know that circles, ovals and semicircles are not polygons because they all have curves.

2 Sort these shapes into order by number of sides, from the fewest number of sides to the most.

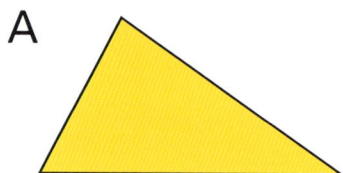

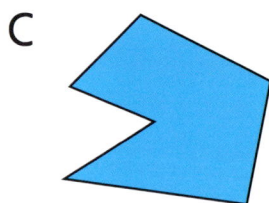

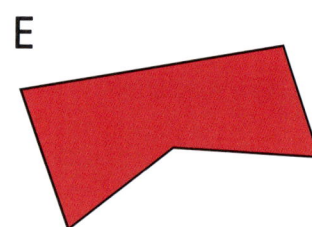

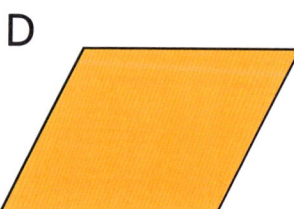

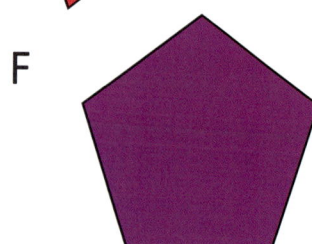

A

C

E

B

D

F

3 Think of your own ways of sorting these shapes into two groups.

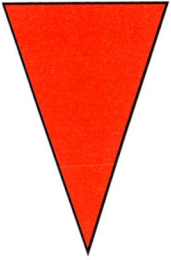

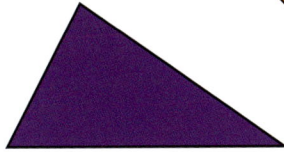

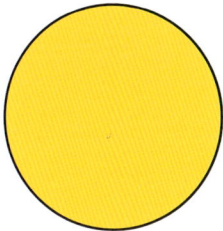

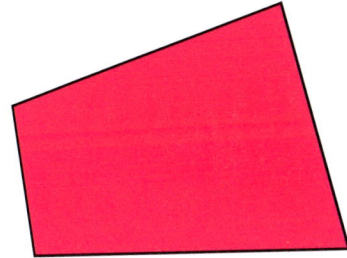

CHALLENGE

I thought of sorting them by symmetry.

There must be lots of different ways to sort them. I am going to find some more.

→ Practice book 2A p153

Make patterns with 2D shapes

Discover

1 2 3 4 5 6 7 8 9 10 11 12

■ ● ◆ ● ■ ● ◆ ● ■ ● ? ?

Complete the pattern using one of these.

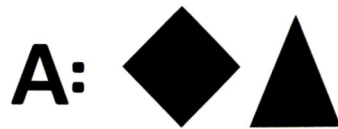

A: ◆ ▲

C: ◆ ●

B: ■ ●

D: ● ■

1 a) Which is the correct choice to complete the pattern?
Is it A, B, C or D?

b) What shape would be in position 20?

Share

a) Four shapes are repeated to make the pattern.

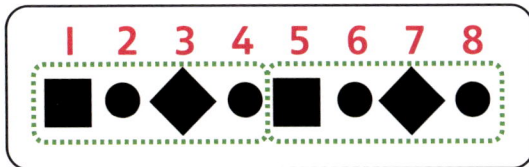

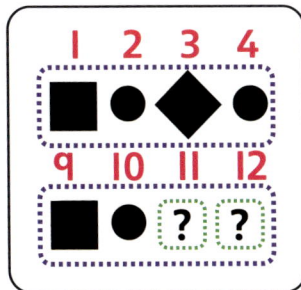

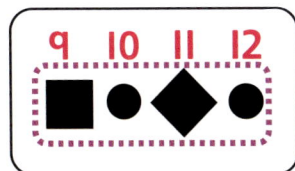

1 2 3 4 5 6 7 8

1 2 3 4
9 10 11 12

9 10 11 12

It cannot be **A** because there are no triangles in the pattern.

I compared the parts that repeated with the choices.

Option C ◆ ● is correct.

b)

1 2 3 4 5 6 7 8
9 10 11 12 13 14 15 16
17 18 19 20

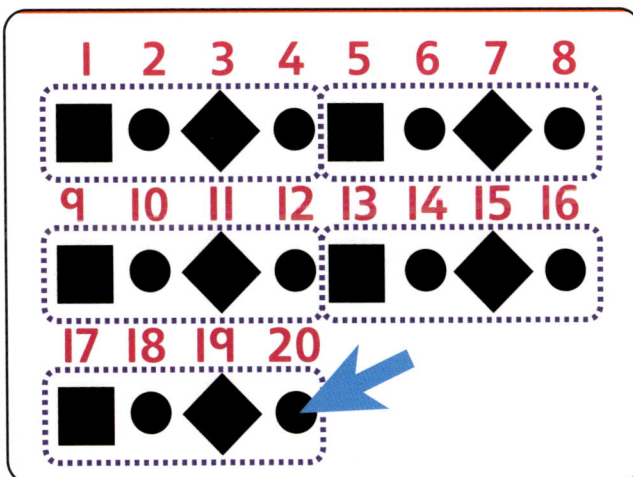

I think the even numbers always have a circle.

The 20th shape must be a circle.

Think together

1 Find the repeating parts to complete the pattern.

What are the missing shapes?

▲ ▼ ▼ ▲ ▼ ▼ **? ?**

> I will first work out the part that repeats.

2 What shape will be in position 15?

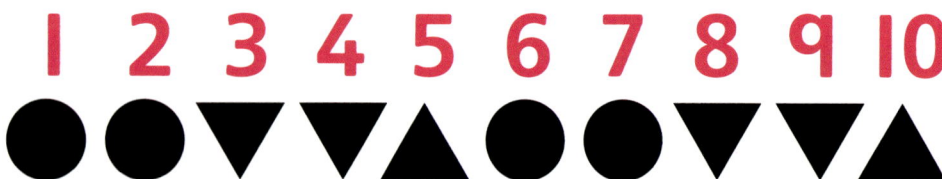

1 2 3 4 5 6 7 8 9 10
● ● ▼ ▼ ▲ ● ● ▼ ▼ ▲

> I will work out the answer for each of the following numbers.

> I think there might be a better way.

214

3 Describe each pattern to your partner.

Draw the missing shapes for each pattern.

CHALLENGE

a)

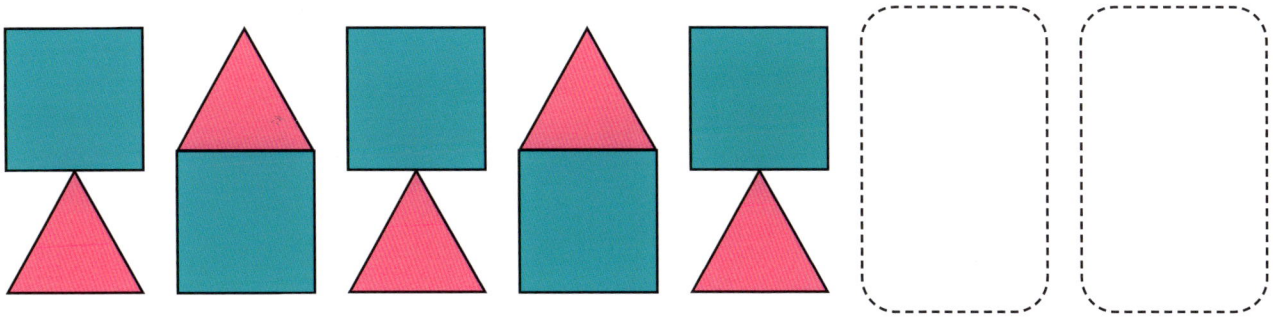

b)

c)

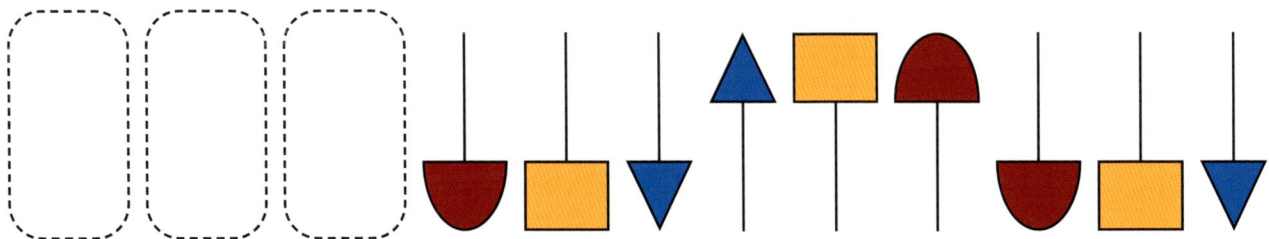

215

→ Practice book 2A p156

Count faces on 3D shapes

Discover

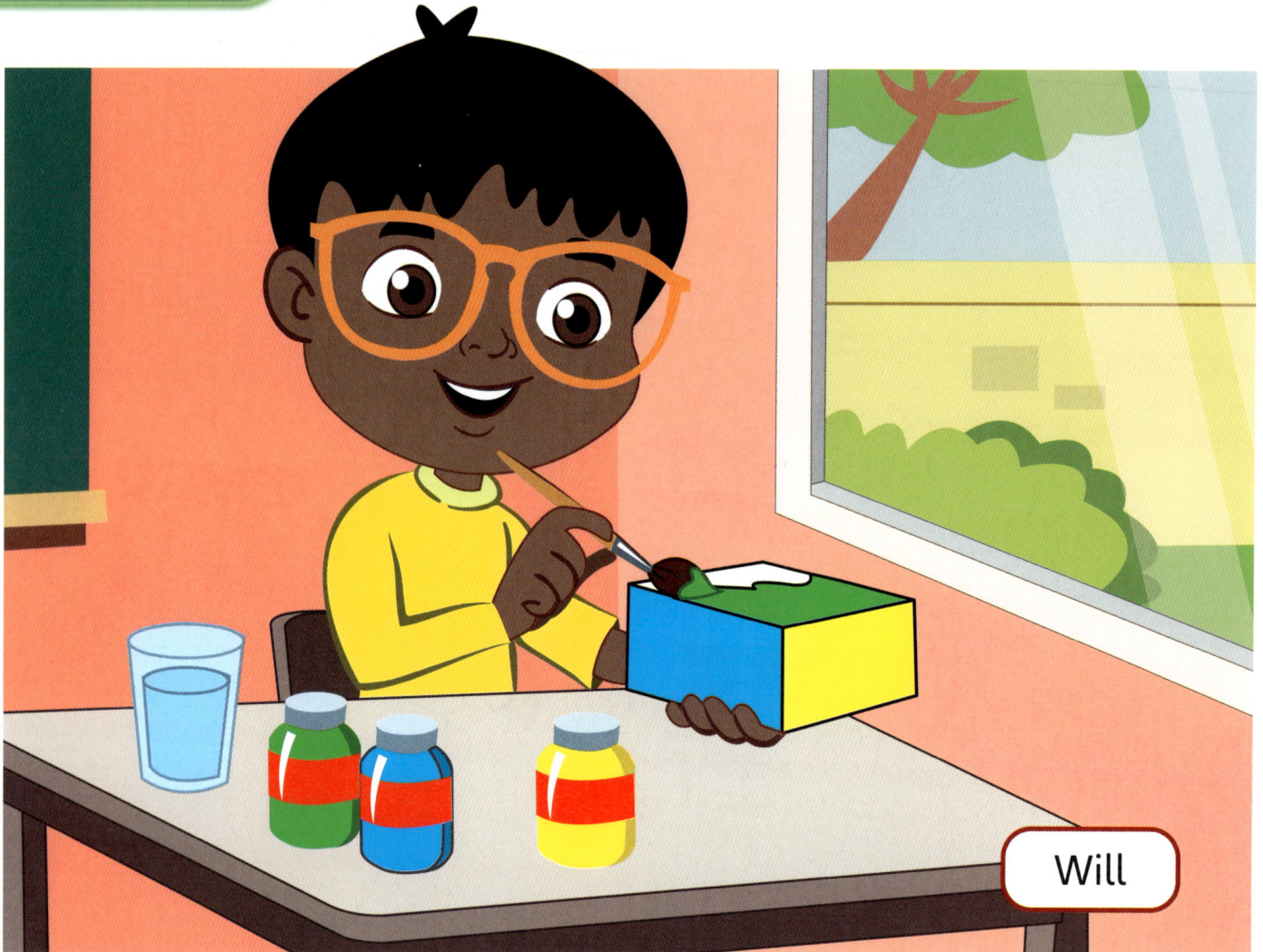

Will

1 **a)** Will wants to paint every face of the box a different colour.

How many colours will he need?

b) Describe the shape of each face.

Share

a) Will's box is a cuboid.

A face is a flat surface on a 3D shape. Each face is a 2D shape.

A cuboid has 3 pairs of faces.

A cuboid has 6 faces in total.

Ben will need 6 different colours.

b) Each face is a rectangle.

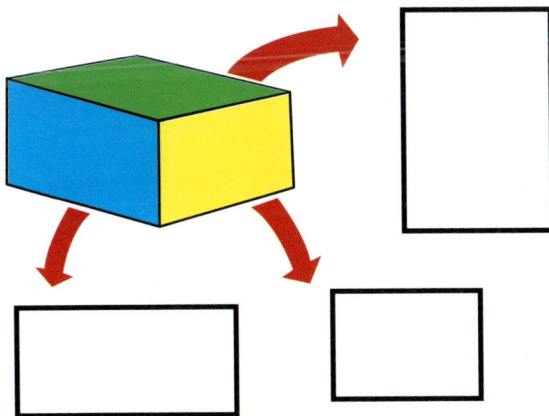

A cuboid can have 2 square faces.

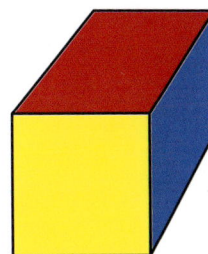

Think together

1   How many faces does each shape have?

2   Anna wants to make a square-based pyramid from construction materials.

> I know that some pyramids have a square base and some have a triangular base.

a)   How many square faces does Anna need?

b)   How many triangular faces does she need?

c)   How many faces will she need in total?

3 How many faces does each shape have?

What shapes are the faces?

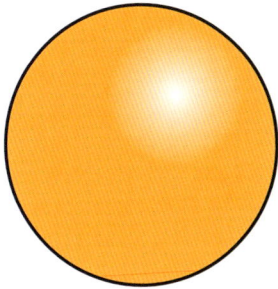

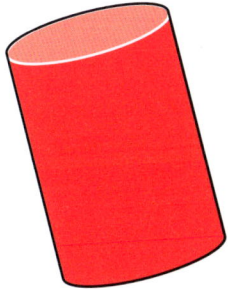

CHALLENGE

A cone and a **hemisphere** have a circular face and a **curved surface**.

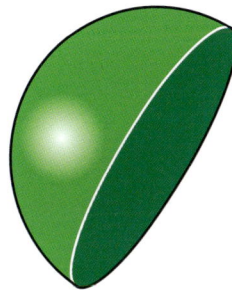

Does a sphere have a face? If I try to print using a sphere, I don't get a circle.

Remember, a face is a flat surface.

219

→ Practice book 2A p159

Count edges on 3D shapes

Discover

Look at my cube!

Molly

Bob

Hassan

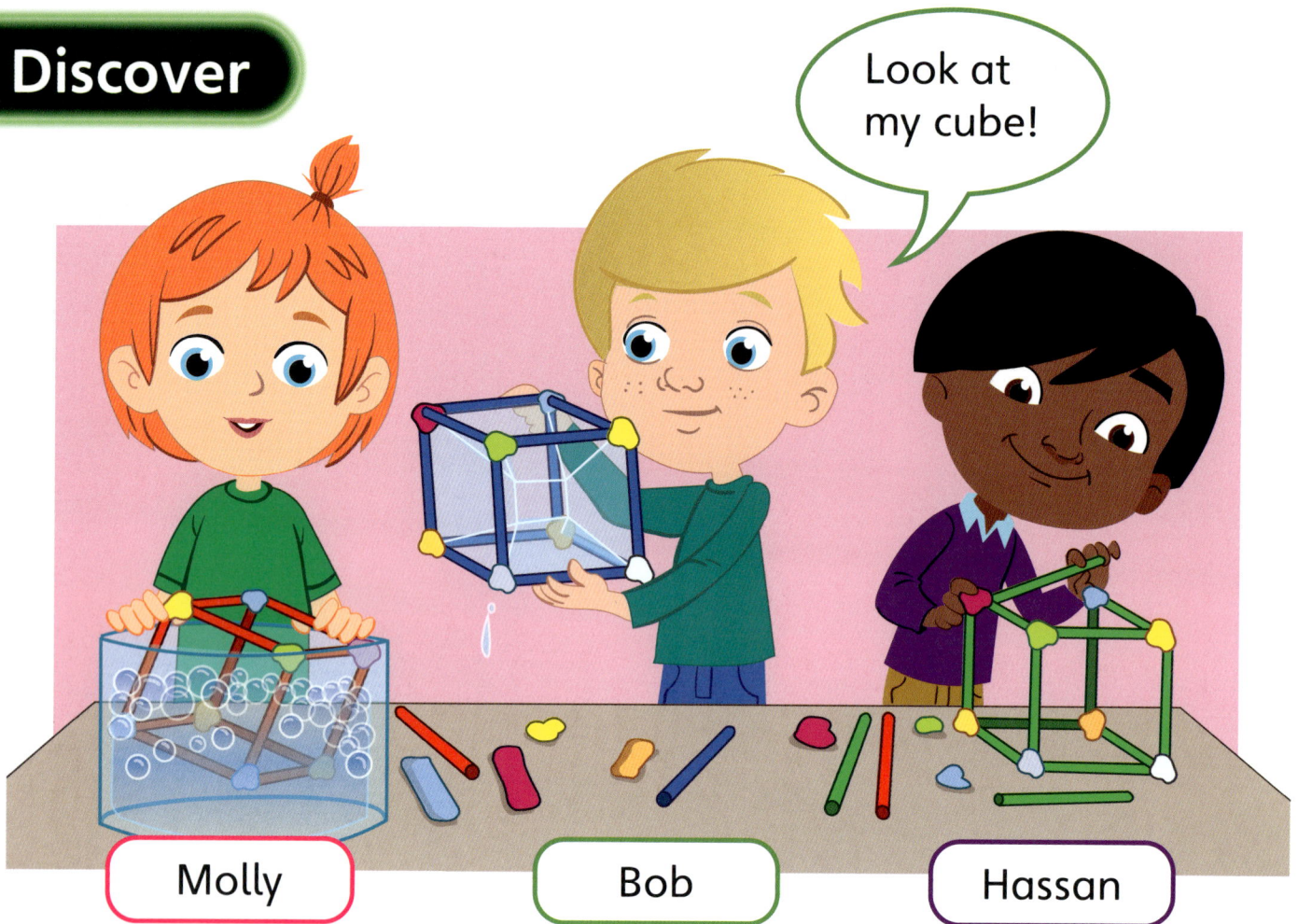

1 **a)** Hassan is making his own cube to dunk in the bubble mixture.

How many straws does he need?

b) There are three different cubes: small, medium and large.

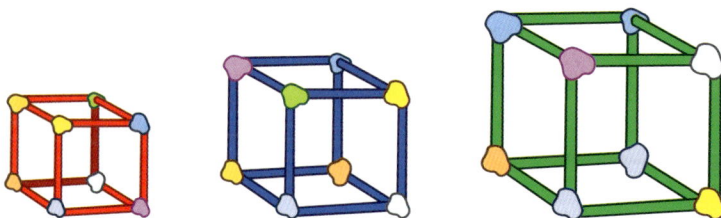

What is the same? What is different?

Share

a) A 3D shape has **edges**.

These are straight lines that are the sides of the faces.

A cube has 12 edges.

In each cube, there is 1 straw for each edge.

Hassan needs 12 straws to make a cube.

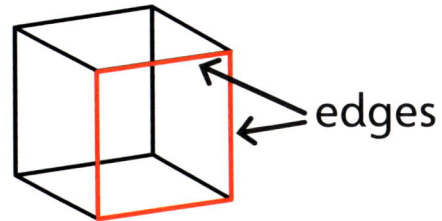

edges

> I counted the edges in order, so I didn't miss any or count any twice.

b) Each cube has 6 square faces and 12 edges. This stays the same.

The length of each edge and the size of each face change between the cubes.

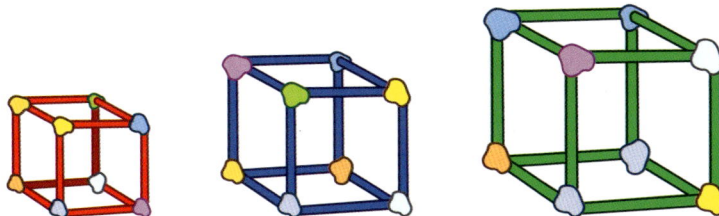

Think together

1 Molly makes different shapes to dunk in the bubble mixture.

How many straws does she need to make each shape?

Shape	Number of straws needed

The last shape has a triangle at each end. It is called a triangular **prism**.

2 How many edges does each of these 3D shapes have?

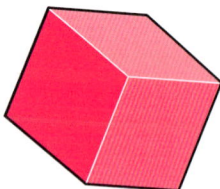

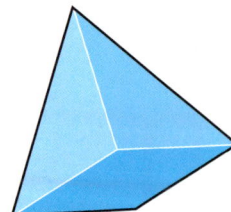

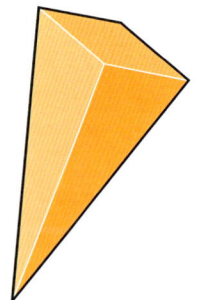

3 Kendi and Abbie are making shapes from construction materials.

CHALLENGE

My cube has more edges than faces.

Does my pyramid have more faces or more edges?

Kendi

Abbie

Does a 3D shape always have more edges than faces?

I will investigate other shapes.

→ Practice book 2A p162

Count vertices on 3D shapes

Discover

I am using sticks and joining tubes.

1 a) Mia is making a triangle-based pyramid.

How many joining tubes does she need?

b) How many joining tubes does she need to make a pyramid like this?

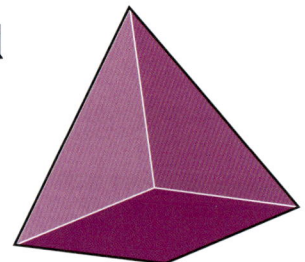

Share

a) Mia makes the base first.

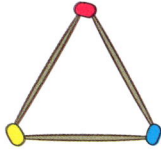

She adds 3 sticks and joins them at 1 vertex at the top.

There is a joining tube at each vertex.

Mia needs 4 joining tubes for this pyramid.

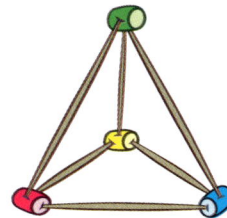

A pyramid with a triangular base has 4 vertices.

b) Mia makes a square base.

Then she makes 1 more vertex at the top point.

A pyramid with a square base has 5 vertices.

Mia needs 5 joining tubes for a pyramid with a square base.

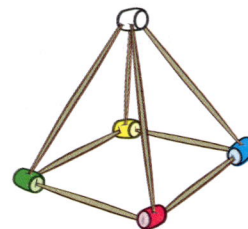

Think together

1 How many vertices does each shape have?

Shape	Number of vertices

Remember that each vertex has a joining tube.

2 George wants to make different pyramids.

Each pyramid will have a different base.

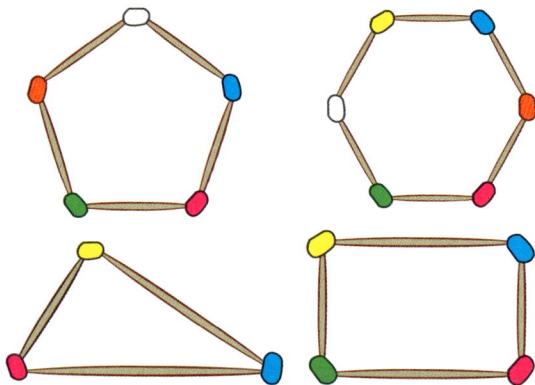

I know each pyramid will have a point as well as a base.

How many joining tubes will George need for each pyramid?

CHALLENGE

3 Darcey has 8 cubes.

She joins them to make one large 3D shape.

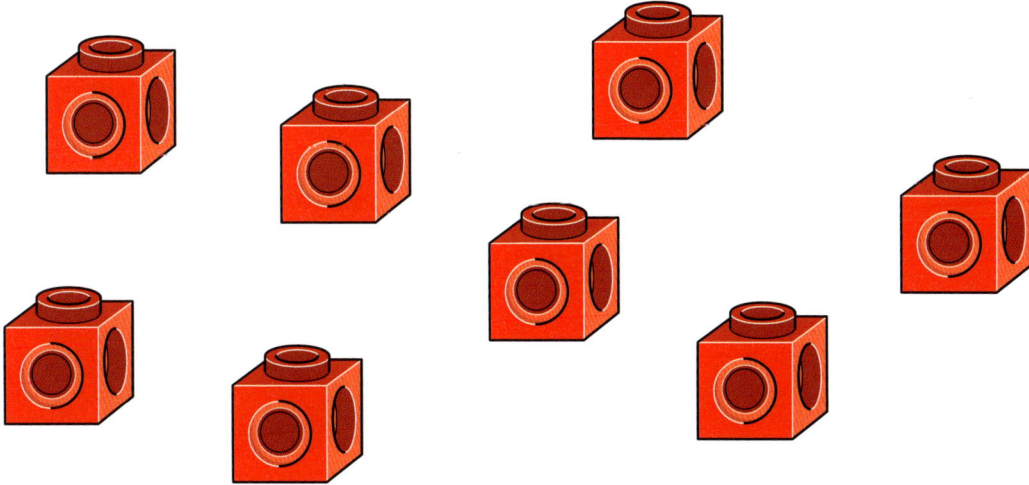

Can Darcey make a shape with 8 vertices?

Is there more than one solution?

→ Practice book 2A p165

Sort 3D shapes

Discover

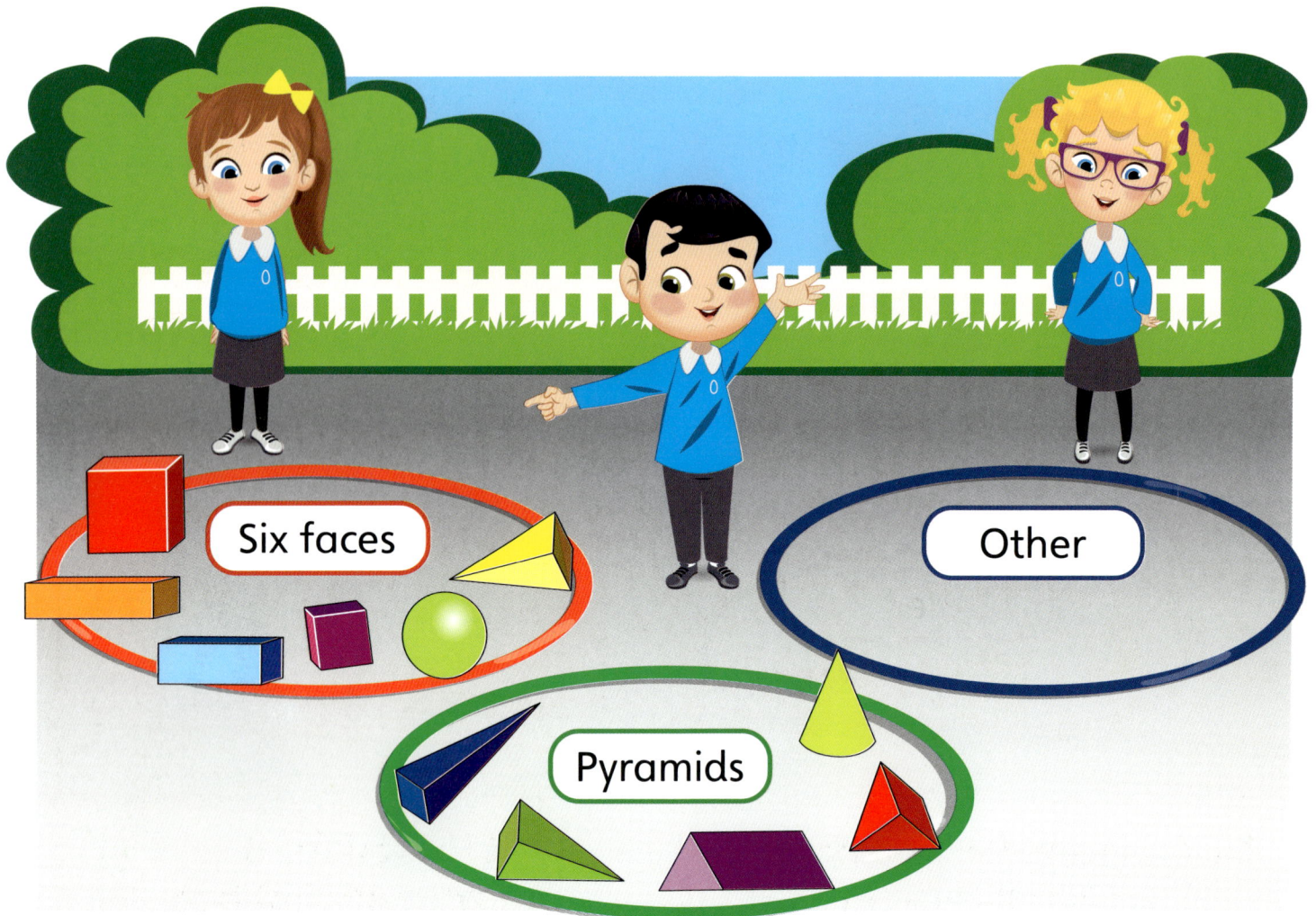

1 **a)** Which shapes are in the wrong place?

b) Can you think of a different shape that could go in both the 'Six faces' group and the 'Pyramids' group?

Share

a) This is how the shapes should be sorted.

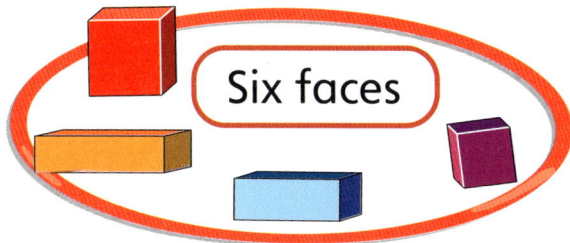

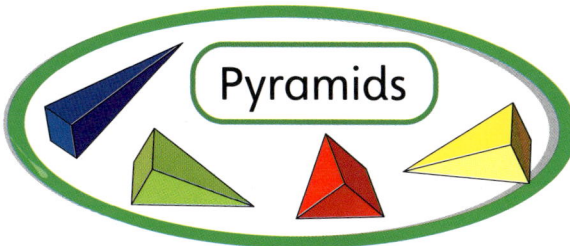

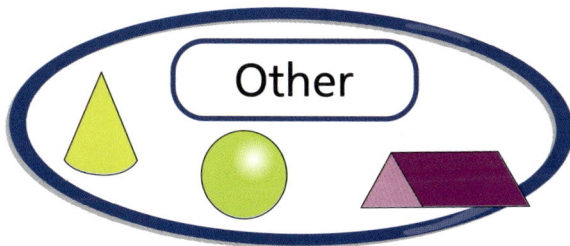

Six faces

Pyramids

Other

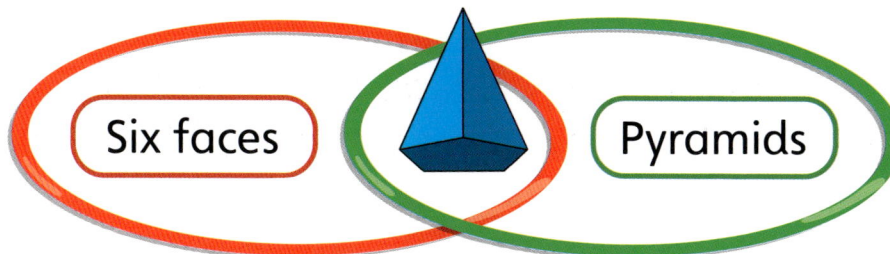

> I know that all cuboids have 6 faces. A sphere and a cone have a curved surface, so I put these in the 'Other' group.

b) A pyramid with a pentagon base has 6 faces in total.

It could go in both groups.

Six faces

Pyramids

> I looked for a pyramid that had 6 faces.

Think together

1 Match the shapes to the number of edges.

< 10 edges

> 10 edges

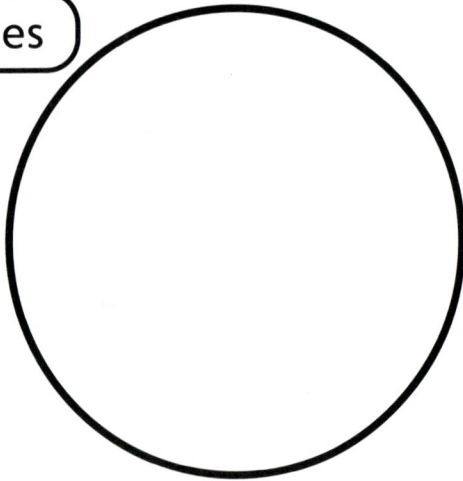
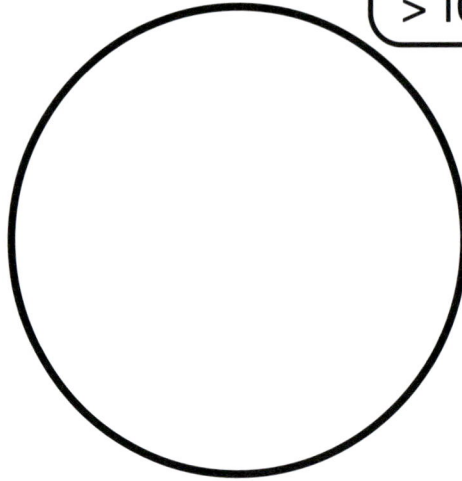

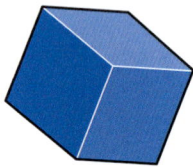

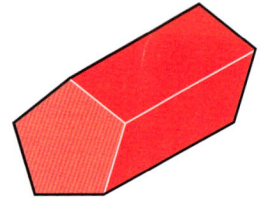

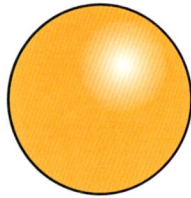

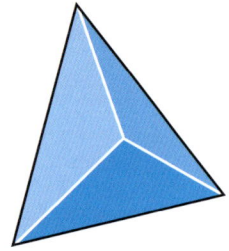

2 Put these shapes in order of the number of faces.

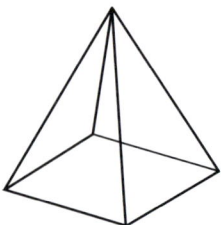
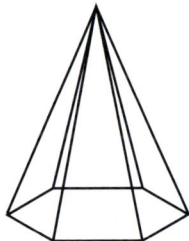
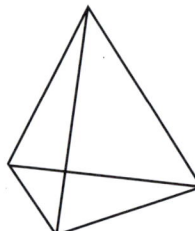
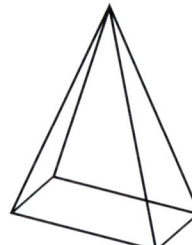
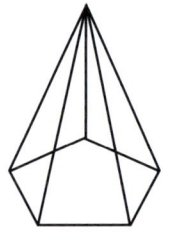

A   B   C   D   E

3 Choose headings to sort these shapes into three different groups.

CHALLENGE

I will make one of the headings about curved surfaces.

This reminds me of when we sorted 2D shapes.

231

→ Practice book 2A p168

Make patterns with 3D shapes

Discover

1 **a)** Describe the pattern of the 3D shapes that Tilly and Josh have made.

b) Create the same sort of pattern using these shapes.

Share

a) The pattern is the same whether you start from the left or the right.

The matching shapes are in the same order from the middle.

It is a symmetrical pattern.

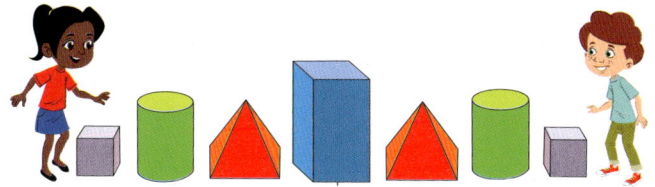

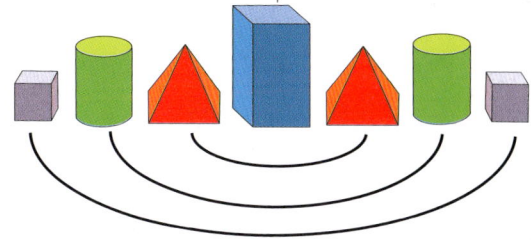

I noticed that the pattern does not repeat.

b) There is only one cylinder, so it must go in the middle.

Then there must be two matching shapes.

Then two more.

Then the last two.

I put the matching shapes in a different order.

Think together

1 Work out the missing shapes in these symmetrical patterns.

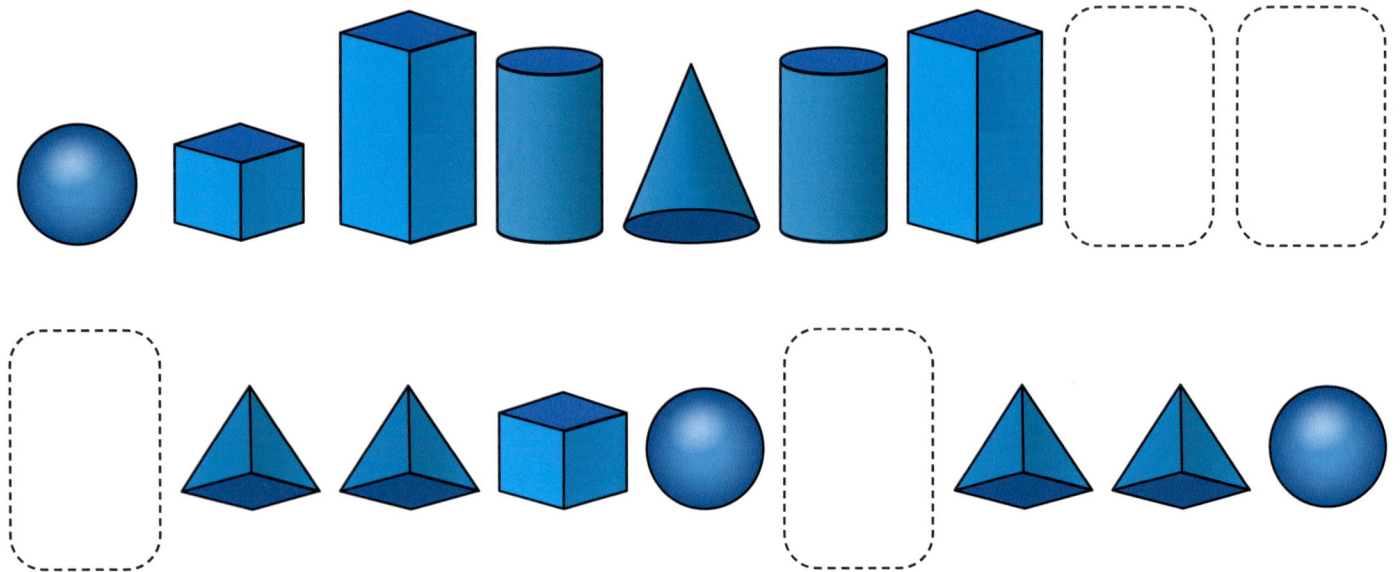

2 Create a symmetrical pattern with these sets of shapes.

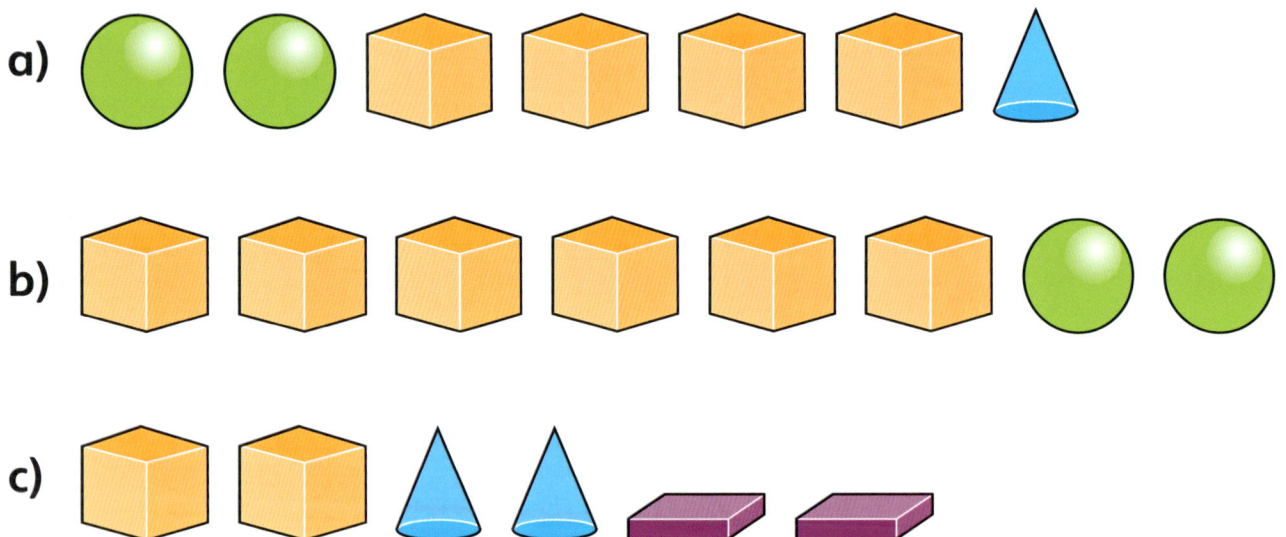

a)

b)

c)

3 **a)** Make a symmetrical pattern with some of these shapes.

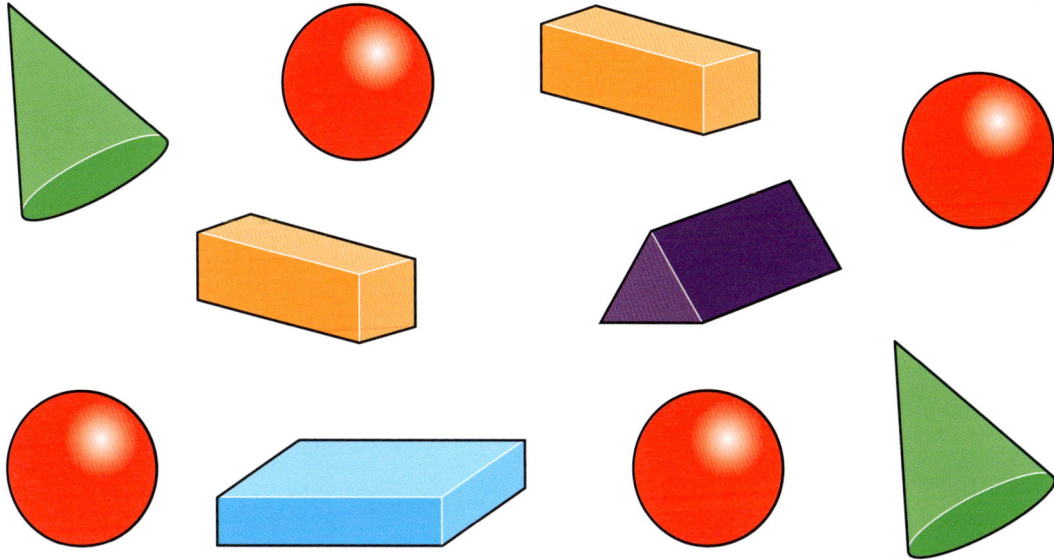

CHALLENGE

b) Make a repeating pattern with the shapes.

I wonder how many patterns I can make.

I will use as many of the shapes as I can in each pattern.

235

→ Practice book 2A p171

End of unit check

Your teacher will ask you these questions.

1 Which shape does not have 4 vertices?

A 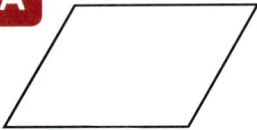 **B** 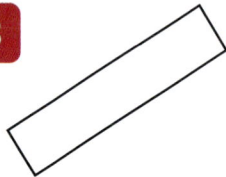 **C**  **D**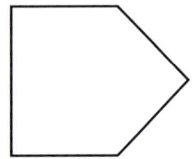

2 Which shape cannot be placed in either of these groups?

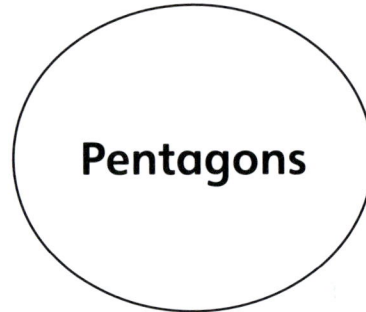

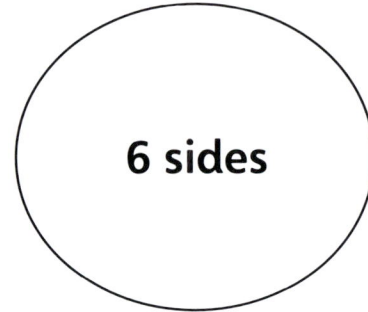

A 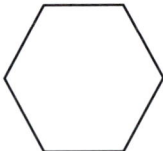 **B** 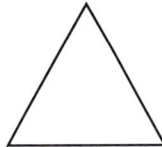 **C** 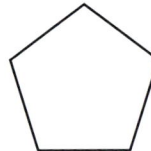 **D**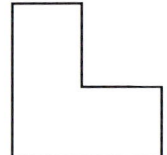

3 Choose the shape that has the fewest edges.

A  **B**  **C** 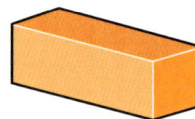 **D**

4 Which shape has these faces?

A 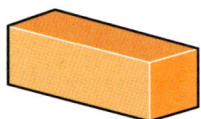 **B**  **C** 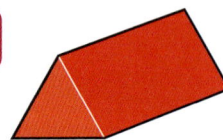 **D**

5 Choose the shape to complete the pattern.

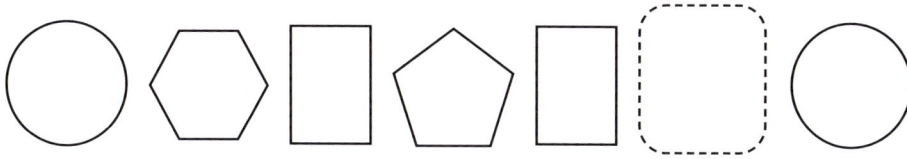

A rectangle   **B** square   **C** pentagon   **D** hexagon

Think!

Theo has a square.

He draws 2 straight lines on it and then cuts along them.

Now he has 3 new shapes.

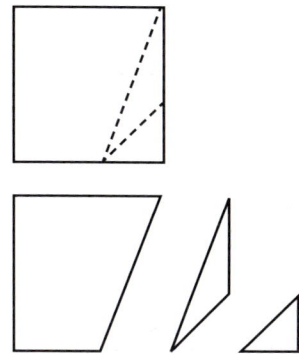

He counts the number of vertices for each new shape.

Find a way to cut the square into 3 shapes so each shape has a different number of vertices.

Is there more than one way?

Describe your shapes to a partner.

These words will help you.

pentagon

vertices   **sides**

hexagon   **triangle**

→ Practice book 2A p174

We have learnt lots and we are ready for next term!

What have we learnt?

Can you do all these things?

⚡ Work with numbers up to 100

⚡ Add and subtract within 100

⚡ Subtract across 10

⚡ Know the properties of 2D and 3D shapes

It's ok to make mistakes as long as you try again!

Now you're ready for the next books!

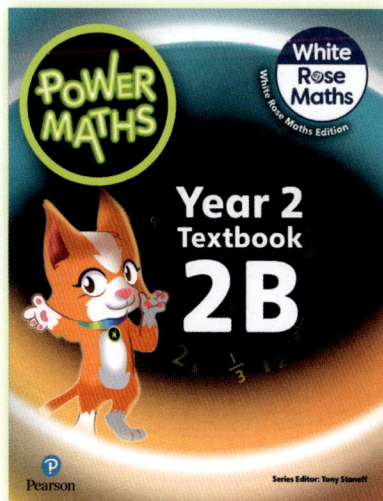

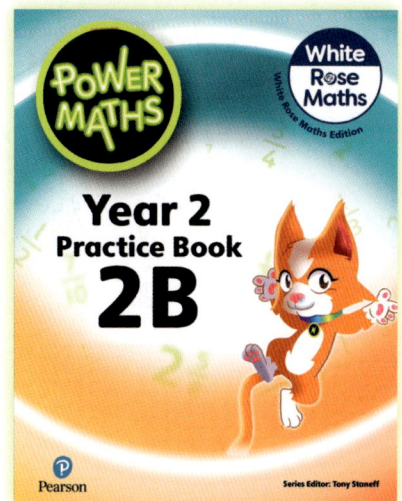

POWER MATHS

White Rose Maths
White Rose Maths Edition

Year 2 Textbook 2B

Pearson

Series Editor: Tony Staneff

POWER MATHS

White Rose Maths
White Rose Maths Edition

Year 2 Practice Book 2B

Pearson

Series Editor: Tony Staneff

239

Published by Pearson Education Limited, 80 Strand, London, WC2R 0RL.

www.pearsonschools.co.uk

Text © Pearson Education Limited 2017, 2022
Edited by Pearson and Florence Production Ltd
First edition edited by Pearson and Haremi Ltd
Designed and typeset by Pearson and Florence Production Ltd
First edition designed and typeset by Kamae Design
Original illustrations © Pearson Education Limited 2017, 2022
Illustrated by Laura Arias, Fran and David Brylewski, Nigel Dobbyn, Adam Linley, Nadene Naude
and Dusan Pavlic at Beehive Illustration; and Florence Production Ltd and Kamae Design
Cover design by Pearson Education Ltd
Front and back cover illustrations by Will Overton at Advocate Art and Nadene Naude at
Beehive Illustration
Series editor: Tony Staneff; Lead author: Josh Lury
Authors (first edition): Tony Staneff, Josh Lury, Kelsey Brown, Liu Jian, Zhang Dan and
Wang Mingming
Consultant (first edition): Professor Liu Jian

First published 2017
This edition first published 2022

23
10 9 8 7 6 5 4 3

British Library Cataloguing in Publication Data
A catalogue record for this book is available from the British Library

ISBN 978 1 292 41970 1

Printed in the UK by Bell & Bain Ltd, Glasgow

For Power Maths online resources, go to:
www.activelearnprimary.co.uk

Note from the publisher
Pearson has robust editorial processes, including answer and fact checks, to ensure the accuracy of
the content in this publication, and every effort is made to ensure this publication is free of errors.
We are, however, only human, and occasionally errors do occur. Pearson is not liable for any
misunderstandings that arise as a result of errors in this publication, but it is our priority to ensure
that the content is accurate. If you spot an error, please do contact us at resourcescorrections@
pearson.com so we can make sure it is corrected.